SOD THIS, I'M OFF TO MARBELLA

SOD THIS, I'M OFF TO MARBELLA

John Roberts

Sport Media

About the author

*John Roberts wrote for the Daily Express
(where he was George Best's ghost-writer),
The Guardian, the Daily Mail and The Independent.
His books include The Team That Wouldn't Die
(the story of the Busby Babes).*

*As Matthew Engel once wrote in the British
Journalism Review: "I suspect posh-paper sports writing
changed forever the day John Roberts left the Daily Express
to join The Guardian in the late 1970s, was handed
a piece of routine agency copy and picked up a telephone
to start asking questions."*

Sport Media

Copyright: John Roberts

Produced in 2010 by Trinity Mirror Sport Media:
Business Development Director: Mark Dickinson. Executive Editor: Ken Rogers.
Senior Editor: Steve Hanrahan. Editor: Paul Dove. Senior Art Editor: Rick Cooke.
Sales and Marketing Manager: Elizabeth Morgan.
Sales and Marketing Assistant: Karen Cadman.
Additional design: Zoe Bevan.

Sod This, I'm Off To Marbella acknowledgements:
Daily Mirror, Daily Express.

ISBN: 9781906802417

Photographs:
Trinity Mirror,
John Roberts collection, Peter Jackson

Printed by
CPI Bookmarque

Praise for the book:

Original book, *George Best: Fall of a Superstar* limited edition published by Derek Hodgson, 1973, was sold in the Manchester United club shop. As it was published, Best had returned from exile and reiterated his desire to continue his United career, prompting many critics to ironically suggest the original book was 'out of touch' in painting its portrait of a fallen star.

'A remarkable insight into George Best's erratic lifestyle'
(Ian Wooldridge, Daily Mail)

'This book is highly readable... without really cutting beneath the surface. This is not Roberts' fault. There is nothing to dig. It shows an intelligent, likeable man who likes doing his own little things in his own time. George Best. Super footballer, yes. Superstar, never'
(Goal Magazine)

'Fall of a Superstar is still not a bad title for a book which captures in fragmentary impressions the life and times of a *once* wayward genius'

(The Guardian)

George Best fanclub letter, 1972

CONTENTS

Introduction

The Best and Best's shadow

100 years has just passed since the opening of Manchester United's stadium at Old Trafford. The ground has provided a stage for some of the sport's greatest players, but it was George Best who revolutionised the public's perception of the footballer as a celebrity.

It is amazing to think that July 2011 will mark the fiftieth anniversary of George's arrival at United as a skinny 15-year-old who immediately became homesick and took the first opportunity to go back to Belfast.

Persuaded that Manchester promised to be the beginning and not the end of his world, George returned to Old Trafford and before long made magic wherever he played.

George's arrival at United in 1961 coincided with the abolition of the Football League's maximum wage, £20 a week at the time, following the threat of strike action by the Professional Footballers' Association. Fulham immediately made Johnny Haynes the nation's first £100 a week footballer.

Although George was never the highest paid player in the land, or even the highest paid at United, what singled him out was his potential to earn a fortune from commercialism, which he failed to maximise.

David Beckham, while lacking comparable ability but with no

drink problems and with sufficient nous to allow himself to be guided to outside riches, might in business terms be described as George Best taken to a logical conclusion

Shortly after George helped Manchester United to win the European Cup at Wembley in 1968, I suggested to the Lord Mayor's office in Belfast that it would be appropriate for the city to hold a civic reception for its acclaimed footballing son. The Lord Mayor agreed.

Northern Ireland has produced many wonderful footballers, and I became acquainted with some of them while working there as the Daily Express sports correspondent. The irrepressible Charlie Tully, whose wing trickery and wit had entranced the supporters of Glasgow Celtic, still brought smiles with his quips ("Some club directors don't know if the ball's blown up or stuffed!") and Bertie Peacock, the great former Celtic midfielder, was managing the Northern Ireland international team and also managing and playing for Coleraine in the Irish League. (Peacock had a bar in Coleraine and one night a visitor said, "You don't know me, Bertie..." Before he could finish the sentence, Peacock interjected: "You're the big mouth from under the clock at Ballymena's ground.")

Peacock had been a key player in the Northern Ireland team guided by Peter Doherty to the quarter-finals of the 1958 World Cup in Sweden, a team of quality and character featuring the cultured Danny Blanchflower and Jimmy McIroy, the hard line of Wilbur Cush, Willie Cunningham and Tommy Casey, and the agile goalkeeping of Harry Gregg, a survivor of the Munich air disaster that took the lives of eight of his Manchester United team-mates in the February of that same year.

What distinguished George Best was that he was a football genius. At 22 he had been essential to United's winning one of the sport's most coveted prizes and at the same time had been voted

BTI 5GS.

14th June, 1968.

Dear Mr. Nicholls,

The Rt. Hon. the Lord Mayor desires me to say how much he appreciated the arrangements made by Mr. John Roberts, your representative in Belfast, for the reception for George Best - "Footballer of the Year" and a native of this city.

It was a most successful occasion and certainly Best enjoyed it very much.

The Lord Mayor has thanked Mr. Roberts, but I feel sure you would wish to learn of his excellent efforts prior to the visit.

Yours sincerely,

Lord Mayor's Secretary

D. Nicholls, Esq.,
    Sports Editor,
        "Daily Express",
            Gt. Ancoats St.,
                MANCHESTER

European Footballer of the Year and the Football Writers' Association Footballer of the Year.

Best's breathtaking talent was encapsulated earlier by his performance for Northern Ireland against Scotland at Windsor Park in 1967. Delegated by Ireland's manager, Billy Bingham, to ensure that Scotland's raiding full back Tommy Gemmell was fully occupied by defensive duties, Best skilfully undermined Gemmell's confidence in the opening phase of the match before creating havoc for the whole of the Scotland team.

On this afternoon Best popped up in every position except goalkeeper, dispossessing Scotland's finest and building attacks with mesmerising ball control and accurate passing. Best would also have scored but for the agility of Scotland's goalkeeper, Ronnie Simpson, who was eventually beaten by the only goal of the match by Dave Clements, completing a move fashioned by Best.

Interestingly, Best was the calmest person as elation filled the Northern Ireland dressing room after the match. While team-mates and reporters raved about his inspiring role in the victory, Best simply smiled, evidently fulfilled by his display on the pitch. In May the following year Best was at the height of his form in a United team that had peaked and was about to go into decline.

In June 1968, in recognition of his accomplishments, Best and his family were the Lord Mayor's guests at Belfast's City Hall where, in an easy atmosphere in his parlour, the Lord Mayor, William Duncan Geddis, presented George with the City of Belfast tie. There were smiles along with applause as George put the tie round his neck and tied it, for George Best wearing a tie was not a common sight.

This was, after all, the man nicknamed El Beatle by a Portuguese journalist following his part in Manchester United's 5-1 victory against Benfica in Lisbon's Stadium of Light in March 1966; the handsome virtuoso with long hair who was to transcend football in his general appeal as a product of the "Swinging Sixties".

Having chatted with George's parents, Dick and Ann Best, during the civic reception, my wife Phyllis and I later invited them to our home, where, over a chicken dinner, we discussed, among other things, what it was like being the parents of a son who had gained such fame since leaving home while at the same time bringing up George's four younger sisters, Carol, Grace, Julie and Barbara.*1 Dick, an iron turner in the Belfast shipyards, met Ann when she worked in a cigarette factory. They lived on Burren Way, on the Cregagh Estate in east Belfast, and appeared easy to get along with. Although Dick played amateur football until he was 37, Ann, a former hockey player, had a superior sporting record.

The Daily Express transferred me back to their Manchester office in September 1968, and three years later I became the ghost-writer of George Best's weekly column while also covering the exploits of the Merseyside giants Liverpool and Everton.*2

Among my souvenirs is a District Bank cheque from Sir Matt Busby for £8, dated 10 February 1969. I joke that I was Matt's cheapest signing and that he let me go because I had everything except pace, strength, stamina, vision and ability. I received the cheque for ghosting Matt's column in the Express one week when his regular collaborator, Bill Fryer, was away.

Another souvenir is a copy of Sir Matt's 1973 autobiography, Soccer at the Top, signed for me "with thanks" for reading the manuscript written by Bill Fryer, copyright Beaverbrook Newspapers, serialised in the Express.

Unfortunately, in January 1969 Matt neglected to mention to the Express that he was going to retire. The first the newspaper knew about it was on the day most of its rivals ran the story. *3

Wilf McGuinness, the former "Busby Babe" promoted from his position as coach to succeed Busby as United's manager, guided the team to an FA Cup semi-final and two League Cup semi-finals during a brief tenure. Wilf made a bold decision to drop Bobby Charlton, a former team mate, for a match at Everton. I was sent to Charlton's home in Lymm, Cheshire, and waited in my car for his return. He invited me inside and, though obviously unhappy about being left out of the team, he was characteristically diplomatic in his public response.

In May 1971, prior to becoming George's "ghost", I was sent to Klagenfurt, Austria, to link up with Manchester United on a post-season tour of Austria and Switzerland. The purpose of my trip was to be close to the team in case a successor to McGuinness as the manager was announced. McGuinness had been sacked the previous December, with Sir Matt returning to his old office to take temporary charge of the team.

My arrival at Klagenfurt on 26 May coincided with Sir Matt's 62nd birthday, and I was in time for a slice of cake and assurances that no appointment was imminent, even though there were rumours that United had their eye on Dave Sexton, the Chelsea manager. (Sexton eventually became United's manager in 1977, leaving Queen's Park Rangers to succeed Tommy Docherty at Old Trafford.)

From Klagenfurt, United moved on to Graz – with Alex Stepney providing entertainment on the coach journey as an impromptu DJ – before ending the tour in Zurich, where they played the Grasshoppers (Denis Law joked that the opposition had scored 100 goals – all headers). Bobby Charlton, who had been to Moscow to play in a FIFA testimonial match for the superb Soviet goalkeeper, Lev Yashin, rejoined the United squad.

Comfortable to have Sir Matt back in charge, even in the short term, and content to face the future one match at a time, the players were in good spirits.

Brian Kidd visited a barber. "How do you like my Luigi Riva cut?" he asked, hoping a new look would contribute to his hitting the net with the regularity of the Italy striker.

As in Klagenfurt and Graz, I joined a group of players for a night out after the match. We were invited to a club, but a doorman stopped me, saying, "You're not a player."

One of the group interjected, "You're right – he's Jimmy Murphy." For one night only, I masqueraded as Sir Matt's assistant manager and nobody questioned that I looked rather too young to have fought in World War II.

Before the start of the season an Express photographer heard that Denis Law and Alex Stepney and their families had been invited to the Pontinental Beach Resort, in Sardinia, along with, among others, Malcolm Allison, the Manchester City coach. The photographer, visualising pictures of Allison training the United players on the beach, persuaded the office to send us both.

Unfortunately, we arrived to discover that Allison had already returned to England to negotiate the transfer of Rodney Marsh from Queen's Park Rangers. So, no photograph. Denis Law was amused. "Well," he said, "you go on tour with United in case there's a new manager – and there isn't – and you come here for Malcolm training United – and he's gone. John Roberts – Non-Reporter of the Year!"

One time I arrived in Sheffield, where Paddy Crerard was due to face an FA disciplinary hearing. Everybody attending the hearing was standing around, waiting for Crerand, who was late. Suddenly a meat wagon pulled up outside the hotel. The doors were opened to reveal Crerand and Sir Matt Busby sitting on boxes of meat. Crerand's car had broken down on the Yorkshire Moors and the driver of the meat wagon had stopped and offered them a lift. After the hearing I drove Paddy and Sir Matt back to Manchester. The Express ran the story under the headline, "Meat and Two VIPs".

When George arrived at Manchester United in 1961, I was the sports editor of my local newspaper, the Stockport Express.

GEORGE BEST
Fall of a Superstar

... is not a story about football. It is about a superb athlete who was generous and charming and who was brought down by a society that was too kind to him.

JOHN ROBERTS

... was born in Stockport in 1941 and was sports editor of the **Stockport Express** at 19. Shortly after his 21st birthday he joined the **Daily Express** and first met George Best during a three-year spell as that newspaper's Northern Ireland sports writer.

When George joined the **Express** as a weekly columnist John was the natural choice to work with him and was in almost daily contact with him during his last two years at Old Trafford. John is best fitted to tell this story of the disintegration of a public image.

75p

GEORGE BEST
Fall
of a
Superstar

by JOHN ROBERTS

Derek Hodgson, Publisher
196, Burton Road, Manchester 20

George Best
Fall of a by John Roberts
SUPERSTAR

Foreword by Kevin Keegan

18

During this time I first came into contact with Denis Law, who was playing for Manchester City. One of Stockport County's players, Tommy Anderson, was living in the same lodgings as Denis, a fellow Scot, at Withington, Manchester, and I went there to interview the pair. *4

By coincidence, my home is a short distance from the white-tiled house George had built on Blossoms Lane in Bramhall, Cheshire, and I was soon given a taste of what trying to keep tabs on him would be like. My office phoned to say they had received a call from a woman who had seen George on crutches at his front door. Making haste to Blossoms Lane, I rang George's door bell and was greeted by one of George's pals, a hobbled, Beatle-haired, unshaven Eddie Hindle – the man who had been seen on crutches. He had broken an ankle.

While this was a case of mistaken identity, you will discover in the following pages chronicling my three years as Best's ghost-writer – when he went from being the best thing since sliced bread to being sliced bread dunked in vodka – that George contrived to send me the wrong way almost as often as he dummied full backs.

This book, priced 75p in its original form, was called *Fall Of A Superstar* and there were only a few copies printed. Because of its controversial nature it was only sold 'under the counter' in the club shop. Hopefully this revised and updated edition will reach more fans and a new generation who can understand more about two of the most significant seasons in the modern history of football in this country and of course, the legend that was Best... and how we coped with having a genius on our hands.

John Roberts

PART ONE
THE LIMELIGHT

'If we say that we have no sin we deceive ourselves, and there is no truth in us.
Why, then, belike we must sin, and so consequently die:
Ay, we must die an everlasting death.
What doctrine call you this,
Che sera, sera,
What will be, shall be?
Divinity, adieu!'

— Doctor Faustus,
Christopher Marlowe (1564-1593)

I

Che Sera

*'Matthews did well considering he had no
left foot, couldn't shoot and couldn't head the ball...'*

*JUNE, 1971. Little Gina Fitzpatrick makes her debut as
a model for a clothing firm whose directors include
soccer star George Best.*

*Her assignment is to parade around in one of the firm's
new shirts for the benefit of George and his fellow bosses.
Not surprisingly, five-year-old Gina, daughter of ex-
footballer Reg Fitzpatrick is a bit bashful at first, perched
as she is on the directors' table in London. The white shirt
looks rather like a baggy midi dress on her. But George
gives her a few tips and she soon starts to put her best
foot forward.*

*Afterwards, they give Gina, from St Albans, a soft drink
and chocolate biscuit to go with her first taste of
modelling.*

***

Manchester United, a tradition rather than a professional organisation, has been through another upheaval. Wilf McGuinness, a
favourite son of Old Trafford where he has played and coached
from boyhood to manhood, a Busby "babe" who had to grow up in

a hurry when injury wrecked his playing career, has gone. He has been judged a failure as a team manager by the directors. Who could follow Sir Matt Busby? Who will follow McGuinness?

Frank O'Farrell is the new hope, having stepped from the relatively peaceful pastures of Leicester City to take on one of the biggest jobs in world football. He is quiet, methodical and offers a more detailed tactical approach to the job, veering away from the Busby way of letting great players play their natural game. But most of Busby's great players have aged and their legacy has not been passed on.

With the new season only five days old, the newspapers on the morning of Thursday, August 19, 1971 do not make happy reading for followers of football or George Best.

Soccer's Violent Night

Goalie hurt in catapult attack
Dozens held: 38 players 'booked'
Rain of pellets at Spurs match
Rival fans clash in Leicester and Exeter
George Best weeps as ref orders him off

At Stamford Bridge, there is plenty of incident. United are the visitors. George leaves the field clearly distressed — he was already under a six-week suspended sentence and received a booking toward the end of last season. But he has no reason to get involved in an argument and is once again the victim of his own touchy temperament.

The incident happens in the 40th minute — just after Chelsea had taken an undeserved lead and United's Willie Morgan had been booked. Best, who had earlier seen a United "goal" disallowed, has clearly reached boiling point.

As Best talks with referee Norman Burtenshaw, United coach Malcolm Musgrove leaves his touchline seat in an attempt to pull him away. Skipper Bobby Charlton also races across the pitch to intervene. Both are too late.

Burtenshaw, underlining the Football Association's new code of conduct, points to the dressing room — and Best sits down in disbelief.

After a minute of confusion he is led away and up the tunnel bv Musgrove. Neither Best nor his manager, Frank O'Farrell comment afterwards. All referee Burtenshaw, from Great Yarmouth, says is: "I'll be submitting my report as usual."

So United go in at half-time without Best and trailing to the goal that started the storm, scored in the 39th minute by Tommy Baldwin after Peter Osgood had risen high to steer a header to him.

But in the second half, United start to play sweetly flowing football. United finally get back into the game in the sixty-eighth minute with a magnificent goal. Left-back Tony Dunne, overlaps down the left, beats one man beautifully before crossing for Brian Kidd to score with a flying header.

Two minutes later. United go ahead. Kidd races through a non-existent offside attempt to round Phillips. The goalkeeper pulls him down and Kidd runs on to shoot into the side netting. But Burtenshaw then awards a penalty and, from it, Morgan strokes the ball home.

It is left to Bobby Charlton to provide the climax of the match with a wonderful goal ten minutes from time.

Just over the halfway line, he accelerates sweetly past two defenders before driving a tremendous shot on the run that rockets into the net from 25 yards.

Chelsea are poor, and offer little threat. But they pull one back in the closing stages when a header from John Dempsey raps the post and Osgood is there to turn the rebound into the net.

Autumn and winter 1971

It is early evening, and in the narrow, glazed brick kitchen of "Che Sera", a white tiled palace in Blossoms Lane, Bramhall, Cheshire, Eddie Hindle is slicing potatoes. Eddie, a brash but likeable fellow with a head framed by dark lank hair and a close-cropped beard, is George Best's companion. George, sex symbol Valentino, ballet master Nureyev and artistic revolutionary Dali of Manchester United Football Club, is still in bed. He is obviously trying to dream away the events of the previous night at Chelsea. Already there are murmurings about a three-month suspension awaiting his return to the capital.

"George likes my chips," Eddie assures me. "He says I could win international caps for making chips. Says I could make chips for England against the Rest of the World."

Eddie opens the door of a freezer cabinet and takes out a pre-packed beef stroganoff to garnish his famous chips. At around six o'clock George emerges from the bedroom wearing a black vest, fashionable flared trousers and stockinged feet. The telephone rings, and George goes back into the bedroom to take the call on an extension. It could be one of a million. But it could be important. A girl, perhaps.

Eddie clucks around like a mother hen complaining that the meal will go cold, and even Eddie's chips do not win prizes when they are cold. He pours from the kind of elegant white and blue teapot you will find at most middle-class high teas in this particular district, 12 miles south of Manchester.

George, his call completed, reappears, and Eddie moves to watch the colour television housed in the wide, imposing white-tiled chimneybreast. George considers his words and talks between mouthfuls of food. "Well, for a start I didn't swear at the referee. I honestly didn't swear at him," he repeats for emphasis.

So what am I doing in George Best's house, interrupting the superstar's enjoyment of Eddie's chips?

I am there because I ghost-write George's columns for the Daily Express. The newspaper had earlier latched on to George's popularity, running a pictorial series, "The Best Set," on its feature pages. This led to the northern sports editor, David Nicholls, assigning me to work with George in producing a weekly column for the sports pages. The columns appear every Friday in the Express and frequently appear on the back page, as George is big news. Following football's biggest star is an eventful task, to say the least.

I leave George to finish his meal, musing that it was only a day or so earlier that he had told my why he did not think he would ever again be in trouble on a football field.

He was convinced that new tighter control on tackles from the rear, in what journalists called a Football Association clean-up campaign, would be his salvation.

"In the past I've landed in trouble because of retaliation," he stressed. "I've taken a lot of 'stick' during a game and suddenly I've lost my temper and had a go back. It's like this: some people are bad tempered and some are not. I must be bloody bad tempered. It's frustration more than anything else. If I am fouled, it's not the pain that bothers me. It's the frustration about a good move being ruined because some clogger has just taken the legs from under you. But this is going to be eliminated to a large extent by new measures. And that will eliminate cause for retaliation."

***

Frank O'Farrell is there. Bobby Charlton is there. Almost everyone who is anyone in football is there. But there is no sign of George Best.

It is Thursday, September 9, 1971 and the occasion is the Rothmans Golden Boots team awards in London. This is the second year running that he has failed to appear.

The word from George is that he is injured. He says: "I have to stay behind at the ground for treatment to my injured ankle. But the organisers have been told about it and I'm sure they know I can't be there."

Francis Lee and Joe Mercer and Malcolm Allison are there from Manchester City. Billy Bremner and Don Revie are there from Leeds. Ferenc Puskas has come all the way from Athens to make the presentations.

"Maybe it is a long way to limp. But George should really have made a better job of explaining that," complains a journalist. 'Missing again' reads one headline the following morning.

***

George, with team-mate Willie Morgan as his star witness and Cliff Lloyd, secretary of the Professional Footballers' Association, his attorney, escapes suspension when the Chelsea case is heard later in London. A Football Association disciplinary commission accepts that it was a case of mistaken identity; that George was really swearing at Morgan, not referee Burtenshaw.

The refereeing establishment complains "we've been made to look like mugs" but apart from a few head shakes here and tut-tuts there, English football heaves a general sigh of relief that Best will stay in the game, accepting that there are too few exciting individual players – ornaments, if you like – to be able to afford jailing the greatest attraction in the game. That is the mood of this time, five years after the elixir of England's World Cup triumph at Wembley. George, now 25, is the folk hero from a council estate in Belfast,

Northern Ireland, who, with a Charles I hairstyle and trendy clothes and tastes, truly reflects the age of prosperous, easy-going youth.

There have been football stars before, but never one quite like George. No Carter, Mannion, Matthews or Finney had so much so soon. George is big business; better known, better paid and better loved than a prime minister.

"Matthews," he says with the mischievous glint of a toddler dropping a family heirloom down a drain, "did well considering he had no left foot, couldn't shoot and couldn't head the ball."

O'Farrell's immediate impact is impressive. United shoot to the top of the First Division, shrugging off the handicap of having to play early home games on away grounds as a punishment for crowd disturbance at Old Trafford.

The club has new potential and the range of George, footballer and tycoon, seems unlimited. On match days he is caught up in it all, enjoying the performance and the reaction it gets like a Punch and Judy man. Once, twice, sometimes three times a week, the crowd, the match, the glory set him apart from basic human endeavour.

He tells me: "I would rather have 60,000 people having a go at me for 90 minutes than play in half-empty grounds. I need the crowds to lift my game. I never go into any game thinking I might not play well. That thought never enters my head. It is not conceit, just confidence in my ability. I do not think you could go out there and do it if you had any doubt about it. I'm not too keen on hanging around dressing rooms. I'll stay outside talking to friends as long as possible, and when I go in I leave it until the last minute to get changed. I don't really suffer from nerves before a game. I just want to get started. I hate to hear the final whistle, because if I'm playing well I want the game to go on forever, and if I'm struggling I want to keep playing until I find my form again."

Outside the House of Commons called the Football League and the House of Lords called the Football Association, the game is accepted as a branch of show business. It has taken time, but people have finally realised that even Sinatra can only fill a theatre to capacity and no more, while thousands more create bulges in a top First Division ground to see the top match or the top personality.

That is the live show. Television lets in millions more, and if it is a case of Top Football v Sinatra in England, I would back Top Football to draw the bigger audience. Soon, therefore, stars of stage, screen, television and radio link up with their cousins in football boots; first as spectators, then as friends.

George's aura, his extraordinary talent and reputation with girls make him football's number one celebrity. If indeed he is the character he is made out to be, then he keeps all displays as an extrovert restricted to the people he calls his friends. Others have to settle for the way he expresses himself on the field and what they hear and read.

But he is forever sought after for public appearances: open this, visit that, shake hands with Self-made Sam, lad, he's the Bore of the Year, you know. George cannot say no.

His way is to smile good-naturedly and say: "Right. Fine. See you then." He just does not turn up, and his absence rarely makes the heart grow fonder.

There are exceptions, and one is Michael Parkinson, television personality and journalist. George has known him since the days of short back and sides (almost) when Yorkshireman Parkinson appeared regularly on Granada television in the north. He likes him and is a guest on his "chat show" beamed nationwide from London. He talks about "The Birds" and says: "When they start to take their clothes off they say things like: 'I'm not doing this just because you're George Best.'" Headlines follow and critics swoop, prompting George's fans to put pen to paper. A 65-year-old grandmother is among those who contact the newspapers. "I think George was pressurised for an answer regarding his sex life so what was he supposed to do? After all, some of the girls do ask for it, don't they?" O'Farrell is not amused by the furore. "George should realise that it's great for someone like Parkinson that he should go on his show and say things like that. It's great for Parkinson, but it's not good for George's image. I have a duty to perform as manager of United. I don't want my only day off spoiled and interrupted by people ringing up and asking what I think of a footballer's appearance on television.

"I have told George that when he appears on TV he has his own name to protect and he should remember that the ripples of these types of interview can affect a lot of other people. I am sure he understands this. But I want to make it quite clear, no matter what impression that TV interview made, that there is no fitter or more dedicated player on my staff."

Two girls win a competition to find a name for the house success built. Many locals sneeringly suggested that with all those tiles it would have to be "Public Convenience", but George's selection was "Che Sera" after the song "Che Sera, Sera, what will be will be". He tells me that the suggestions struck a chord deep down, reminding him of his late maternal grandfather, George Withers, after whom he was named.

"Grandad Withers was my hero when I was a boy in Belfast. We went everywhere together," says George.

"He died the day I was due to sit my 11-plus examination at school, so everyone tried to keep the news from me knowing how upset I would be.

"Anyway, before I went for the exam I called at a sweet shop where someone said: 'Sorry to hear about your grandad' and had to tell me. I didn't go to the exam that day and my parents eventually found me sitting on the pavement, still crying my eyes out.

"I remember one time Grandad Withers took me on holiday when 'Che Sera' was the big hit song. It seemed to be played everywhere we went, and ever since I've always associated it with him and with that time." *5.

II

The Chaps

'Teach us to number our days.'

"Che Sera" is home from home to George's friends every Sunday. To the world outside they are the hangers on, moths attracted to his spotlight. To George they are "The Chaps", and he has been known to fret if one should be late or fail to turn up for a Sunday soiree. A man chooses his own friends just as much as they choose him, and I have been greatly impressed by George's signs of loyalty towards those close to him.

On those occasions when George has been a fugitive they have done everything possible to cover his tracks, and when, it seems, the world has caught up with him and is about to envelop him in a mass of newspapermen and curious, over-eager bystanders, the "hangers on" have hung on well, shielding their man, organising discreet, deceptive getaway cars. They have become George's bodyguards with an efficiency that would have made Al Capone envious.

George resents talk that "The Chaps" live off him and are a set of confidence tricksters sticking close to a willing victim. His anger mounts as he discusses these attitudes, saying: "I don't care what people say about me. They can say what they like. But they are always trying to get at me by having a go at my friends. I've been a First Division footballer for eight years and a lot has happened in that time. I know enough to be able to sort out the people who are genuine from the ones who are just out to exploit me. I'm not the bloody fool people seem to think I am."

"The Chaps" often can be found around an area of Manchester city centre known as The Village: Bridge Street, Motor Street and King Street West, off Deansgate, down by the side of Kendals' store.

Motor Street, a short road facing St Mary's Parsonage and running between King Street West and Bridge Street, houses George's boutique, Edwardia[*6] adjoining the Village Barber. Directly in front of the shops there is a small open plan private parking and dropping off area, where George's E-type Jaguar sometimes stands and his agent Ken Stanley's Rover 3500 Coupe appears when business arrangements – or problems – need to be sorted out.

Turning left at the barbers into Bridge Street you can see some fine examples of Victorian architecture, the lower parts of which have long been converted into shops. One such building on the right bears evidence of the stone mason's craft in the words Street Children's Mission. Farther along is a pub, The Bridge, and the Sawyers Arms is on the corner of Deansgate, some 25 yards from the splendid neo-gothic John Rylands Library with its collection of some of the most significant books and manuscripts ever produced.

Facing Bridge Street is John Dalton Street, leading up to Albert Square and Manchester Town Hall, where United celebrated the 1968 European Cup triumph. The clock faces on the Town Hall's imposing central clock tower are inscribed: "Teach us to number our days."

Eddie Hindle is from Salford, an ambitious lad determined "to make it on my own". He is an agent dealing in trendy men's wear, but first met George when he was working for a time behind the bar of the Brown Bull,[*7] which is at the bottom of the hill from the Village. Malcolm Mooney is lean with a thin face and drooping moustache. Like the others, he wears his dark hair shoulder length. He runs George's boutique, Edwardia, in the Village.

Malcolm Wagner could be taken for Mooney's brother, though he is shorter and wears extra-large spectacles. He is the Village barber and has tended George's locks for years ("a medicated shampoo three times a week, a touch of dandruff treatment on the rare occasions it's needed and a general shaping of the style once every month to six weeks").

There are others I see less frequently, like Danny Bursk, a Manchester United devotee who invariably chides me: "Why do you blokes keep writing those things about George? Why don't you leave him alone?" I try to explain that it is because George is a public figure. He smiles and shakes his head and we agree to differ.

The weeks flow in a barely changing pattern because, despite his jet-set image, George is basically a creature of habit. When he is not playing or training he can be found usually around the boutique, in the barber's or at home.

At home, more often than not, means a girl will be calling or one is already there, will soon be leaving and another is likely to be on her way by car or taxi. Evenings also stick to a general pattern: a public house called The Grapes, which is to move. It is a cosy place with music-hall charm on Deansgate. Soon it will be around the corner in Little Quay Street, buff-brick modern, but remaining cosy, friendly and noisy, with a busy sparkle inside. Mine host is Billy Barr, an American, who has a nice line in jovial, easy-going patter. He gets on well with "The Chaps".

The centrepiece of The Grapes is a large rectangular bar, where many of the regulars congregate on stools. There are also tables for drinking and dining. The clientele is a mixture of business people and a younger crowd. On one occasion George is at the bar with the Daily Express northern editor, Robin Esser, the northern sports editor David Nicholls and me. On the far side of the bar is a sports writer from another newspaper, who writes about us: "They seemed to be enjoying George's company much more than George was enjoying theirs." This seems a bit rich considering the writer was there romancing a woman who was not his wife.

After a visit to The Grapes, George and "The Chaps" usually move on to a nightclub. A favourite is "Blinkers", and not only because it is located only a few yards around the corner from George's boutique. "Blinkers" is a sophisticated discotheque owned by one of George's friends, Selwyn Demmy, a Manchester bookmaker. They get on well enough for Selwyn to join George on some of his sojourns to Majorca. The "Blinkers" motif is a pony club cartoon, and the chiefly fairly affluent members are the Cheshire set, a few footballers and one or two other celebrities. The women are in mini-skirts or midi-skirts and all drink, dine, or dance to the beat of songs such as Norman Greenbaum's Spirit In The Sky, Freda Payne's Band Of Gold, Smokey Robinson's Tears of a Clown, Dawn's Knock Three Times, and T Rex with Get It On.

Annabell's, off Albert Square, is also popular with George and "The Chaps", and here again the routine is familiar: George drinks vodka and lemonade and stands with his friends away from the crowded dance floor. He likes places where he is known, accepted and gets least trouble from the constant stream of admirers, well-wishers, back-slappers and face-slappers.

The boys are all casual, with black or patterned fitted shirts or skinny sweaters, and flared pants. No ties. "One night," Eddie says, "we are all on our way into a club when someone lets in George and tells the rest of us we can't go in because we haven't got ties. George comes out again and says: 'If you don't let them in, you don't let me in.' It didn't happen again."

Sunday at "Che Sera" is something different, as Malcolm Wagner explains: "Jet Set? You'd laugh at that description if you saw us on Sundays up at the house. We're just like a family. All the lads roll up and George's housekeeper, Olga, has prepared food the night before for us to have for lunch. Afterwards, just like everybody else everywhere else, we watch the match on the telly, watch the film on the telly, and play cards, table tennis or snooker. For dinner we usually go to the Mandarin Chinese restaurant at Wilmslow, then back to the house in time for Mike Parkinson's chat show on the telly.

"I've known Mike a long time. I used to cut his hair. I was the one who persuaded him to let it grow." George takes up the story: "All the lads and their wives or girlfriends go back to the house, and when the television show is over we usually start great debates about every subject we can think of. We get a wide variety of opinions, too, which is hardly surprising because usually there is me, an Irish Protestant, another lad who's a Catholic, plus one or two Jews. You should hear us! But you know what? It's always very interesting."

***

Malcolm Mooney has seen the fingers point, tongues wag and eyes accuse. "I know what they say about us. They call us parasites," he says. "But it's what you know that counts, not what people think or say. I first knew George long before he was well known.

"I don't want to sound like George's public relations officer, but you've got to admire the bloke. Even though he plays for Northern Ireland, who rarely achieve much, and not England, who are the big thing, he is known all over the world. People knock the clothes he wears and his way of life. But he rides it all and still comes out on top. He has the talent, you see."

George is amused about a special assignment he gave to Mooney. "It all started one day when I was in a restaurant in London and a girl passed by the window. I said I fancied her, and before I knew it one of the blokes I was with shot out of the door and brought her in. She was a great-looking bird.

"Anyway, it turns out she's living in Switzerland – with a baron! Before she goes I give her my telephone number, then forget all about it. A long time goes by, and one night I'm on my own at the house when the phone rings and there she is, calling from Switzerland and telling me what a hard time she's having with the baron and how she would like to see me. I tell her to come over, but she says the baron is jealous and wouldn't let her, and in any case she hasn't got the money. She asks me to go over there, but I say I can't, but tell her to leave things with me.

"Anyway I tell all this to Malcolm and ask him to fly to Switzerland to see her and give her the money to come over here. It's all James Bond stuff, and Malcolm agrees. So off he goes, and I'm at home every night waiting for the phone to ring to keep in touch with what's happening.

"Malcolm books into a hotel and sets off looking for the apartment block where the girl lives. It takes a while, but when he gets there he plays it cool and hangs around outside the place waiting for a girl who fits the description I gave him to go into the building. After a long, long while he spots a girl he feels sure is the right one and approaches her. He's wrong, but she does know the girl he's looking for and gives him the room number.

"Malcolm goes up to the apartment, rings the bell, and the girl answers the door. She has seen Malcolm with me and vaguely recognises him. She sort of says: 'Oh', a bit surprised like, and Malcolm looks over her shoulder and sees the baron near the window.

"He's asking who's at the door and Malcolm, quick as a flash, makes out that he's an American student who's a friend of a friend and has been asked to look the girl up and say hello.

"The girl catches on and keeps the act going, and before he leaves Malcolm manages to push a card with the name of his hotel on it into her hand.

"He goes back there and waits for her to call. Eventually she does, but sounds worried and says the baron has not really been fooled. As soon as Malcolm left, he says: 'That fellow is from George Best, and that George Best is here, in Switzerland, isn't he?' She sticks to the story, but he still suspects. So she tells Malcolm to tell me she'll get in touch with me. I haven't heard since. Perhaps the baron has done her in!"

Malcolm Mooney is soon to leave the boutique and, with his French girlfriend, Dominique, later his wife, opens the Borsalino French bistro in Hale Barns, Altrincham.

I do not see much of him after this, though George is there for the opening of the new venture. "Malcolm said he did not want me to invest money in the restaurant because I had put the money up for the boutique. He wanted to do this himself," says George.

Malcolm has a special menu printed with George's name on top. It is George's personal menu, and any meal, at any time, is his for the asking. For life, says Malcolm. I ask George what he would select if he was having a meal there and then, and he says: "Onion soup, veal stew, baked potatoes and butter, followed by cheese and biscuits." Perhaps Malcolm* [8] wins international caps for his baked potatoes.

Friends are fine, but what about a wife and children?

George loves children, and tells me he would love to get married and settle down with the right girl. "But finding the right girl. "That's the thing," he says.

III

Private Lives

'Later, when people asked the girl about George she would say:'George Best? Who's he?"

The United players have just finished a training session at The Cliff, with O'Farrell and coach Malcolm Musgrove concentrating on blocking tactics with defenders, and shooting on the run with the forwards. Denis Law, that other larger-than-life player, is relieving the monotony with Danny Kaye antics. Denis, one of the most exciting players the game will ever see, is also a natural clown. He is also a family man all the way down the line. "I sometimes envy Denis for this," says George.

"He's always the same. As soon as the game is over or at the end of a training session, he goes home to his wife and kids. It must be great to be able to do that." Law's success in separating his public life from his private life is summed up by his wife, Diana's, usual response to day-time telephone calls from reporters: "Denis is at work." * 9

Olga and Fred look after "Che Sera" and, as far as possible, make sure George has all the home comforts. Olga is the daughter-in-law of Mary Fullaway, George's landlady in Chorlton, Manchester, from the time he arrived in town wearing his first pair of long trousers as a 15-year-old, through the formative years on and off the football field right up until the building of his house. George often calls at the old place in Chorlton for dinner after a Saturday match at Old Trafford.

Olga is the housekeeper. She lives nearby and arrives each morning to awaken George and tend to the house. She is wary of callers, conscious of the demands thrust upon George when he is away from football. In this respect Olga is almost protective, checking "if George is in" and, if he is, whether he wishes to be disturbed.

Often, Olga brings along her 18-month-old son, David, who amuses himself while she goes about her work. George will pause, ruffle the boy's hair, smile and say: "Hi there!"

Fred Cook is as old as this century, though you would not believe it to see him at work or running from the house to the car across the road to fetch tools or plants or heavy bags. He is the gardener and general handyman, and George says: "Fred is the fittest man I know. You ought to see him lift great heavy things or just keeping busy. He never stops from the time he arrives to the time he leaves."

Fred has spent most of his life in and around football and footballers. He has been groundsman at both Manchester United and Manchester City, and has spent a great deal of time looking after the gardens of United's club houses. One day he will prune for Sir Matt Busby, another he will take a special plant up to Bobby Charlton's. Fred also has his own market garden in Cheadle Hulme, not far from "Che Sera", and a section of his land is taken up by an impressive stretch of lawn made up of divots Bobby Charlton has collected for him from football grounds all over the world. Pride of place goes to a piece of old Wembley. "You can see the difference. Look. It's beautiful," says Fred.

Fred has known most of the great footballers of Manchester. He once played against City's and United's Welsh wizard Billy Meredith, one of George's artistic forerunners. "It was a charity game at Northwich Victoria, and Meredith was amazing. One of his tricks – and I don't know whether he would get away with it today – was the take the ball up to a full-back out on the flank, push it past him and run over the touchline, out of play, and onto the pitch again to meet the ball at the other side.

"I remember in the game against Northwich he took the ball to a corner flag, and worked it inside, beating players all the time right the way inside the penalty area. Everyone tried to take up positions or move in again with tackles, but he just kept on dribbling until he reached the penalty spot. Then he paused with the ball right on the spot, stepped back, and shot the ball into the net. That's the only time I ever saw a man score a penalty when it hadn't even been awarded."

In more recent times, Fred recalls the day he decided the goal-mouths at Old Trafford were so worn and scarred by battle that it was time to re-turf them. His helper was a groundstaff boy called Eddie Colman, that wonderful player with a wiggle in his hips who was killed in the Munich air crash. "We took the turf we needed for the job from outside the touchline, Eddie set about the job with a cutting tool. We only needed a narrow strip, but Eddie kept find-ing pennies that had missed the big sheets carried round the ground for charities and had lodged in the soil. Eddie collected a real pile, and I told him to keep them as a bonus."

Fred is the man who moved Manchester City's Maine Road pitch, and left it 18 inches farther away from the main stand than it was originally. "The only one connected with the club who knew about it was Freddie Tilson, who I confided in. But some postmen who used to stand at the same place on the terraces every season spotted the difference and asked me about it. The idea was to save too much wearing of the touchlines. I would move the pitch over by 18 inches one season and back again the next. When I eventu-ally left Maine Road the pitch just happened to be 18 inches away from the stand."

Working for George is a varied occupation. "He doesn't have

much to say to anybody, and rarely talks much about football. I like to have a little chat to him when United have had an away game, but conversations never go on for long. But he can be very generous with his possessions. He has often let me take all his trophies, the European Cup medal, Footballer of the Year trophy, caps and everything, to put on show at charity events," says Fred.

There are girls, of course. "Often I'm the one who drives them home," says Fred. "Sometimes they chat a lot. Sometimes they go the whole journey without saying a word. I remember one girl in particular. She used to see George a lot and would come up to the house and cook a meal or just be there when he arrived. It went on for quite a while, until George decided to kick her into touch. He wrote a letter and sent Eddie with it from town to a smallholding just down the road from the house. Then he rang me and told me to meet Eddie at the smallholding and take the letter to the girl at the house. But he said he didn't want her to keep the letter. That I should take it as soon as she had read it, and destroy it. Olga was there, too. I gave the girl the letter from George, and when she read it she was upset and cried on Olga's shoulder.

"While this was happening I was able to get the letter back, and got rid of it. Later when reporters and people asked the girl about George she would say, 'George Best? Who's he?'

"It was funny really."

***

Rumours suggest George is not interested in the boutique so much as a business, more because it attracts plenty of girls. One of my colleagues has heard that the changing room cubicles and the upstairs room are used for more than trying on clothes.

One day George receives a telephone call at the boutique from a girl who says she is Shakira Baksh, the former Miss Guyana.

"Shella", sultry star of a coffee advertisement on television, now married to actor Michael Caine.

"Shella" says she is doing a modelling job in Nottingham and invites George to a party. He asks if there is a quick way of checking whether "Shella" is indeed working in Nottingham. I telephone "Shella's" agency in London and they say: "No, she is working down here." I tell George that his "Shella" is a hoaxer, probably a sun-tanned Nottingham lass looking for a bit of Saturday Night and Sunday Morning.

Girls telephone offering themselves for dates, or write, enclosing a photograph, often ending their letters of undying love with words like: "I am yours for the asking" and "tell me when I should come up to the house and see you". Sometimes the words are more direct, suggestive and accompanied by obscene drawings.

"Look at this," George says, showing me one particular example. "It's written as though it's from a woman, but I'll bet it's from a man." How does he react to this kind of thing?

"It's funny, isn't it? It's a joke." Every so often a rather lumpy, grubby parcel arrives at the house. "Amazing," says George.

"Full of all sorts of stuff. Big sweaters and things. Even underpants. An old woman keeps sending them."

An old armchair is found in George's garden, and George asks Fred to get rid of it. Then his imagination starts to work. "Look," he says. "Somebody's thrown this thing over the fence and probably thinks it's a big laugh. Well, how about putting in my column in the Express something like this:

'My gardener, Fred, came running up to the house all excited the other day. He'd found what looked like a battered old armchair in the garden. But, on closer inspection, he found fistfuls of fivers stuffed in the upholstery.'

"Then when he's had a week to sweat about it, we can put in the next column something like:

'About the armchair, it was just a joke.'"

Sometimes the approach is menacing. "I was in a pub in London with some friends and just before closing time this geezer came at me with a glass. He tried to get at my face, and would probably have succeeded if my friends hadn't got in his way and got me out of the place. I just can't understand that kind of hate. How can you hate someone you don't even know? There are other times when people try to give me aggravation when I can give as good as I get, and it amuses me a bit the way they carry on. A girl came up to me when I was with friends at a night club. I'd never seen her before, but she said: 'I always promised myself that if I ever met you I would slap your face.' I looked at her and said: 'Go ahead. But if you do I'll pick you up and throw you through that bloody window.' She didn't bother."

There is a message to contact promoter Jack Solomons who, to me, is still the boxing Czar with the Churchill cigar and Randy Turpin beating Sugar Ray Robinson for the World middle-weight title. "I'd like you to have a word with George Best for me," he says. "I'm organising a big sporting function to be held in the presence of the Duke of Edinburgh at the World Sporting Club in London. Only the top competitor of each sport will be invited, so it is vital that I know exactly who will be coming even before I send out the invitations. It's got to be right. George is the man for soccer, but I'd like you to ask him if he will be able to come. The position is this: I'd rather him say no right now than let me down later. OK?"

George is with a few of "The Chaps" having coffee in a café called "Mr Strone's", near his boutique in the Village when I tell him what Solomons says. "Oh. Well. Let's see," he says, and considers. "Now, that week Northern Ireland are playing in Belfast on the Wednesday night, so put it this way – if the Irish Football Association agrees to let me go over to London on the Monday and I can then report to them on the Tuesday, I'm interested. See what they say first."

I say: "Well, George, it's quite an honour isn't it?" And he says: "Yes, I suppose it is." So I ask: "Have you met royalty before?" and he makes a mock frown and says: "Oh, that's what you mean...

"No – I mean it's an honour for the Duke to meet me!"

IV

From Russia
Without Love

*'Number 11 ... Best! A roar of approval goes up and even
people on Gorky Street know George is playing'*
,

George, his agent Ken Stanley, Express northern editor Robin
Esser, sports editor David Nicholls and I lunch at the Midland
Hotel Manchester, and discuss George's weekly column. I meet
George at the hotel reception and we go to an elevator. Inside is a
big, dark man holding a bouquet handed to him by a woman. He is
American country and western singer Johnny Cash. We make the
short journey to our floor in silence. I look at the two characters
alongside me, consider what they must be worth in terms of
money, and suddenly the Midland Hotel is more like the Midland
Bank.

Everyone wants George.

He is at the height of his fame and regularly turns down large
cash offers to make personal appearances at shops and nightclubs.
A supermarket chain offers him more than twice his weekly earnings from football to visit their stores, from Lands End to John
O'Groats if he can find the time. George thinks about it, but says
no to about £400 a trip.

When George travels other than for football matches it is for
pleasure rather than business or, at least, a mixture of both. He
often goes to London on his day off from United. He has been
known to fly down for a lunch date and return the same day.

One time George tells me: "I've had a night out with Jimi Hendrix's former drummer Mitch Mitchell".

"It does him good to shoot off like that now and again. It gets him away from everything for a few hours, and relaxes him. He feels better for it," says Eddie.

***

George shoots off to Russia in September 1971. He is to play for Northern Ireland in the European Championship and though a few of the 234 million people in the USSR are in ignorance of his visit, 6,464,000 Muscovites are making up for them. He has never been before, but everywhere he is recognised and out come the autograph books.

There is an English businessman on the flight to Sheremetievo airport. He is a jolly fellow who becomes more jovial by the minute, helped by a swig or two from the bottle of whisky he is carrying. On arrival, as we squeeze into the bus carrying us from the plane to the terminal building, he is close to George and offers him a swig from his bottle. George smiles and takes just a sip to please him. The man is bold, nervous or simply courting disaster. He lines up in the wrong queue as we file along to the passport checkpoint and tries to joke with Russian army officers, who react with good humour and are perhaps wary of his intoxicated capitalist capers.

George asks an interpreter what restrictions there are on bringing in literature. "I've got a couple of Solzhenitsyn's books with me," he explains. "I heard he was banned in Russia so I thought he must have said something worth reading. Anyway, as soon as I ask this geezer about books and tell him what I've brought he just shuts up and walks away. He doesn't want to know."

George looks bored. Russia without love?

I ask him what he thinks of Moscow.

"Terrible." The girls? "No, just the place."

The hotel Rossia is colossal, an enormous rectangular building with 3,000 rooms and 6,000 beds. Our neighbours are The Kremlin and St Basil's Cathedral, and the local radio service piped into each room gives out with a bar or two of "yo-ho heavo" with every time-check.

My room faces the street but I call on a friend for a nightcap and as he pours I look out at lighted windows way in the distance. "Looks as if there are one or two parties in those flats," I venture. "Flats? Flats?" he says. "Those are not flats, it's the other side of the hotel!" Some place.

We are ready to leave for the match, but the coach is still waiting outside the hotel. "We're waiting for one. Guess who?" says Terry Neill, the Irish player-manager. George.

We can see him patiently signing autograph books.

Eventually he strolls away from admirers and joins us. A crowd has gathered outside the Lenin Stadium, waiting for a glimpse of George, the long-haired, rich football player from another world. Inside the atmosphere is building. The people have not come to see the Russians. They have come to see George.

As Jack Milligan, a great character who wrote about sport for the Daily Mirror in Northern Ireland with experience and feeling, once put it: "When George is with us we are somebody."

I think the man on the stadium's broadcasting system graduated by announcing The Beatles. He knows how to build up a show.

"Ireland – number one, McFaul; number two, Craig; number three, Nelson; number four, Nicholson; number five, Hunter; number six, O'Kane; number seven, Hegan; number eight, Clements; number nine, Dougan; number 10, Neill." Then he stops and lets a few seconds go by.

"Number 11..." He stops again, and the atmosphere is electric. "Best!" A roar of approval goes up and even people walking along Gorky Street know now that George is playing.

George does his best to live up to his reputation with a dummy on the left and a shot that whistles wide of a Russian post, a dribble past three men and a gesture of handing over the ball to a Russian defender who is late with a tackle.

I am prodded painfully in the back and turn to see a large, formidable Russian gentleman. "Your Best," he says. "I like him", and I am relieved I have not done anything to offend the man.

The Irish are holding their own, but two minutes before half-time Neill is judged to have tripped a Russian forward and Muntyan, their number seven, scores with a penalty. It is the only goal of the game.

I later get George's thoughts on his Russian experience for his column. "Rather dull," he tells me "with more sad faces than laughing ones." Suspicion of the food out there has led to the squad eating "steaks, steaks, steaks" he reveals gloomily and adds, "Manchester and Majorca are more my taste!"

It has been a memorable experience but my last hours in Moscow are hectic and worrying. A colleague has followed the example of the businessman we met on the way over. Champagne cocktails by day and vodka by night is a fairly potent combination, and we almost miss the plane home.

I frantically help to pack his suitcase, we settle the accounts, and he dashes out of the hotel and throws himself across the bonnet of a passing car, believing it to be a taxi – which it isn't. After we do find a taxi and ask to be rushed to the airport, my colleague tries to make the driver go faster by tossing cigarettes at him as an inducement. For once, George is not the last person aboard.

V

The Eternal Triangle

*'Have you ever wondered why someone would
hate you enough to kill you?'*

George uses his speed, spontaneity and incredible individuality as a scalpel on the defence of Sheffield United, the team that has stepped up from the Second Division and blown raspberries at the established order in the First. George's move starts in the middle of the field. He glances up to study the possibilities open to him.

A pass and run? A long ball to the flank?

A through-ball to a fellow forward?

No, George strides out and runs in a wide, elegant arc towards the right of Sheffield's goal. Defenders move with him, attempting to cut off his line of supply and force him wide into a position where a cross would be intercepted and a shot would be near impossible. George is oblivious to their efforts and ends this run of sheer poetry with an angled shot inside the far posts. He turns, his face a picture of smiling triumph.

In that moment, he is fulfilled. "I had an advantage over their defenders because I knew exactly what I was going to do. They could only guess," he says.

I am talking with Eddie Hindle on the telephone. Manchester United are still confounding those who predicted hard times for O'Farrell. Eddie is raving about George's performance in a match at Stoke City. "Did you read Eric Todd in The Guardian? Fantastic.

He said: 'Best was in much better fettle. He repeatedly had the Stoke defence in the proverbial tizzie.' What a night! Some friends from Sweden were there, and George was full of it. He said to one of them: 'Now do you believe I'm as good as they say I am?'"

George tells me he thinks football would be more entertaining if there were more "mischievousness" on the field. "It needs more fun, more characters," he says, "players who are prepared to do something a bit different."

The strife of Northern Ireland, which has nagged at George as it would anyone whose family is living in a land of such bitter turmoil, eventually knocks on George's door. His life is threatened. Police keep a close watch on him. George is told that if he plays for United at Newcastle he will be killed. The threat is anonymous, but real enough to George and those around him.

He plays at Newcastle, well enough to score yet another winning goal. But the threat triggers off a sequence of events that niggle George, and prompt him to launch an attack, using a ballpoint pen as a sword.

George writes his column for the Daily Express. Usually I discuss a subject or subjects with him and then type his thoughts, to be presented in the form of an article. This time, encouraged by "The Chaps", he actually puts pen to paper with the willpower of Dickens, on the breadline, tackling The Pickwick Papers. "I don't know whether they'll think it's good enough to use, but here it is," he says, adding: "I enjoyed doing it, but I had to force myself to finish it. I was sitting at home, dying to go downstairs for a game of snooker, but I managed to resist the temptation long enough to get it done."

The original is reproduced on the following pages. Apart from two grammatical corrections (changing "whom" to "who" on page three of his work and "it was her" to "it was she" three times in the rhetoric on page four), the Express prints it verbatim.

Have you ever wondered why anyone would dislike you enough to kill you. I've been thinking about it this week after a few cranks had decided to finish me off.

After reading a few things about myself this week I decided if I believed them all then I would have to agree I really am ~~very unlikeable~~ not a very nice person

Mind you I personally don't believe everything I read.

Lets start at Newcastle where it all began. After the match which we won 1-0 I was very interested to read that some of the N'castle players claimed that I had shouted "leave it" when I scored the goal, which put them off. I deny the charge. I've heard of ~~teams~~ teams ~~of~~ blaming their own defence but never the opposing forward. I could just imagine the N'castle defence sitting round in the dressing room after the game thinking which one of

us was to blame and then deciding why
not all deny responsibility and blame Besty
Anyway their allegation could have lead to
30,000 or so N'castle fans not taking so kindly
to me. So there's 30,000 ~~N'castle fans~~ who don't like me for
a start

Then we move on to the Derby game
against M/cr City and a combined effort
between Malcolm Allison & Francis Lee We'll
get Malcolm out of the way first. He claimed
that for our second goal I handled the ball,
but just to make sure he claimed I handled
not once but TWICE. Amazing out of 64,000
fans ~~22 players~~, 2 linesmen a referee and a few hundred
policemen he was the only one who saw it

And now to Francis Lee who imagined
I 'took a dive' when he was booked. I
must also have imagined the cuts and the
bruising on the back of my legs

So I suppose on top of the 30,000 N'castle
fans you can add 35,000 City fans. Not bad
going for a fortnight.

An interesting point for anyone who saw the Francis Lee incident while he was demonstrating the perfect dive. Someone suggested he wasn't showing how I had done it but was in fact trying for another penalty.

After that things quietened down a bit and I was doing very well until Wednesday of this week and then I decided it really was 'have a go at Best' week. I was glancing through the papers in the morning when I came across an article about Miss Susan George. Miss George is an ACTRESS whom some people think is going to go places.

She was being interviewed by a well known columnist when my name cropped up and she very kindly explained to him that when we knew each other ~~it was I who was doing all the chasing~~ all the passes came from me adding the nice little note ~~that~~ 'How can ~~anyone~~ a boy be interested in anybody else when he is so interested in himself.'

Somewhere along the line she forgot to mention

that when we meet it was her who invited me to the studios to watch her rehearse it was her who invited me to stay with her parents and when I went on my holidays it was her who sent me a telegram saying she was arriving a week later. Here details I suppose.

In a funny sort of way. I suppose its a bit of a compliment for a famous <u>actress</u> like Miss GEORGE to be still discussing you with people when you haven't seen her for three years.

If you think I've gone on a bit this week I just thought it might be nice to hear my side of the story.

I don't want my Mum thinking I'm a bad boy all the time.

With the connivance of The Chaps, a journey to London brings George face to face with Eamonn Andrews, the host of 'This Is Your Life'. George is modelling clothes when Eamonn, book of life in hand, surprises him and takes him off to a studio where family and friends are waiting to piece together a story of success.

After Sir Matt Busby and Frank O'Farrell appear, Eamonn digresses from the football.

> *– Eamonn: Now, George Best has followed football success with fame as a businessman, model and sex symbol, to become one of the most talked about men of Britain*
>
> *(Film clips of random interviews with girls are shown)*
>
> *– 'Very good looking. He's not pretty-pretty, as a lot of men are' says one.*
>
> *– 'I think he's a very handsome young man,' giggles another with a trans-Atlantic accent.*
>
> *– 'Oh, he's lovely' sighs a third*
>
> *– 'He dresses well, he's rather nice looking and he's great at sport,' says a more mature woman*
>
> *– 'I think he's marvellous!' The final comment from a matronly type causes laughter in the studio*

More humiliation follows. A story is recounted how George lost his heart to the student nurse that looked after him on Ward Four of the Ulster Hospital in Ormeau Road, Belfast when he was just

11 years old and having his tonsils removed.

> *– Eamonn: Then you knew her as nurse Ruth Anderson. Today, she's Mrs. Ruth Daniell, and we found her at Shanklin Hospital in the Isle of Wight, where she is nursing officer. You've not seen her since you were 11. Well, she's here to see you tonight: Ruth Daniell! Well, Ruth, it's true to say that it came as quite a surprise to you to find out what happened to that little boy from Ward Four, didn't it?*

> *– 'It certainly did. I'd absolutely no idea until you told me that this same boy was the famous George Best, the world wide football player' says Ruth*

> *– Eamonn: But did you know that he'd fallen for you?*

> *– Ruth: Well, come to think of it, he was a chatty little lad and after he was discharged from hospital he sent me two letters signed 'with lots of love'*

George's first team manager at Cregagh Boys Club, Hugh 'Bud' McFarlane, is introduced to tell a tale as is Eric McMordie, the fellow United hopeful who travelled with George as a 15-year-old when he boarded the Ulster Prince bound for a new career in England.

Next, landlady Mrs Fullaway reveals how his favourite dish was Steak Diane before other guests emerge, some obscure and others less so, brother Ian Busby Best the last to walk on to the stage before Eamonn utters the immortal lines...

George Best, This Is Your Life!

I catch up with George for his column to ask him about the show and he says, "This Is Your Life stopped me in my tracks, and I still can't believe Eamonn managed to sneak me from a mock-up fashion show on to his TV programme. I'd always said it could never happen to me without my knowing beforehand but it did and I must say it was a wonderful experience."

***

The American Budd Schulberg, author of the boxing classic The Harder They Fall, writes about Muhammad Ali/Cassius Clay and calls him "The Fifth Beatle". George is the sixth. His looks, mannerisms and attitudes reflect the mood of his time.

He does not have Ali's size, verbal power or gigantic personality, for George says it all on a football field and his actions always speak louder than his words.

But, like The Beatles and Ali, he has captured the imagination of a public who adore ornamental extensions of their egotism: living, breathing idols of sport and showbusiness.

George drives a dark blue E-type Jaguar powered by a V-12 engine and says extra speed can be a greater safety factor because you know when you are overtaking there is always the zip to take you through without lagging. He tells me there are times when he appreciates that he is better off than others and does not take for granted the fact that he is the idol of millions.

"I might be driving home from a training session when the sun is shining and the sky is clear and blue, and I feel good the way you do after a good training session and a bath or a shower. Suddenly I might pass a group of men working hard on road repairs, and it strikes me that this is their working life, day in and day out. That's when I realise how well off I am and how good life has been to me," he says.

Ken Stanley is the agent, the middle man between the sporting arena and the rich rewards of the world outside. Ken negotiates on behalf of the England World Cup squad, cricketers and a host of footballers in offices high in St George's Square, Huddersfield, Yorkshire. Fame becomes big business. Ken, with son David and accountant John Lamb as co-directors, has built an organisation designed to take the weight of business pressures off leading sportsmen and at the same time make money for all concerned.

Ken is a dapper, sprightly man with the quick, keen eye to confirm that he, too, has been a top sportsman in his own right. Table tennis was his game – or "Ping" as he calls it with the affection one might use when recalling the pet name of some old flame – and Ken was an English champion and international. Like most, he is biased towards the merits of his own game and its players. "Bergmann," he purrs. "Now there was a player. There was a sportsman. Talk about speed. Talk about reflexes. Talk about stamina. Talk about pressures. You've got the lot with 'Ping' and it's you against someone else and you have to rely on your skill and you pay for your mistakes. Bergmann was fantastic."

Ken attacks business with the enthusiasm that made him a "Ping" champion, and shows at least as much dedication to his work as the men he represents do to their sports. He is a Lancastrian, and his Yorkshire empire had humble beginnings as a sideline in days when he worked for Mitre sports goods.

He saw Denis Law as a commercial proposition when the electrifying Scot was playing for Huddersfield Town, and it was Denis who suggested that the young George might give Ken a call. "I've been around and done a lot," says Ken. "I've had a five-a-side soccer hall in Burnley and when I started representing sportsmen I did everything from home until the sideline became bigger than my job. But even with Denis I only had a phone. It's all a question of growth. You turn over once with a profit and then work at it so

Gentleman
George:
Setting the
standards

In full flow: Against Wolves, August 1971

Danger man: On free kick duty in a 2-2 draw at Anfield in September, 1971

Ticket to ride: Sir Matt Busby accompanies Best to London for an FA discliplinary hearing after his sending off against Chelsea in 1971

You silly boy: Busby's expression says it all (below right) while (inset left) in happier times as George picks up the Ballon d'Or in 1968

New man in charge: Frank O'Farrell meets Pat Crerand as Denis Law and Sir Matt Busby look on, above. Left: Advertising the Best boutique with recording star Don Fardon in March, 1970

My shadow: John Roberts of the Daily Express with George and wife Phyllis

Bachelor pad: Toasting Che Sera, football's first superstar lovenest

Personal hairdresser: One of 'The Chaps', Malcolm Wagner, adjusts George's hair before he shoots a commerical in Hyde Park, London

At work and play: Looking after some 'investments' at Che Sera, above.

Guests: Housewarming party with Lionel Blair, Yutte Stensgard, Susan Blair and Imogen Hassal in February, 1971

Leaving home:
The end of an era
as George sells Che
Sera for £40,000 to
an Irish businessman

GB and Miss GB: Driving girlfriend Carolyn Moore to the station after a controversial weekend in January, 1972

that next time you turn over it has doubled. Exploitation? There is nothing wrong with the word. I exploit you, you exploit me, everybody exploits everyone else. It's a good word. But it's the way you exploit these things that matters. You've got to do things right. The image has got to be right, for the man, for the game and for us. You've always got to work on sound business lines. Either you can or you can't. Either you will or you won't, either you do or you don't – can-can't, will-won't, do-don't; it's as simple as that."

There are times when George can but won't, when appointments are broken and the road to becoming a millionaire footballer is littered with discarded contracts.

Other times George can and does. Then, out come the suits, the boots and the camera crews. He is shot at from every conceivable angle time and time again: when you've got him, make the most of it.

"Some of the men I meet, heads of big firms, are golf lovers," says Ken. "And some of the golf lovers are not interested at all in soccer. I can tell just by their reactions when I am talking to them about George that they would be showing much greater interest if I was talking about Arnold Palmer. But I can always say: 'Look, get all the people who work for you out in the car park or somewhere and say Arnold Palmer has come to say hello to them. Then tell them George Best is here. Now, who do you think would get the most response from them, Arnold Palmer or George Best?' Then we can get down to business. The image must be right for George. For George it must always be Rolls Royce."

Ken has another way of putting over a point. He uses the triangle to symbolise the structure of soccer. It is his pet analysis of the game, but to George it is Ken's eternal triangle. George has been through it, base, sides and apex, time and time again at lunches with prospective buyers of The Name. Ken will take out of his pocket a piece of notepaper, or use whatever is available to draw lines and explain: "The base. That's your schools football and all the millions of boys coming into the game year after year. The sides. That's your Football Association and your Football League and your players at amateur, local league, part-time professional and professional levels. And then there's the apex. Your top-class players. The big names. The World Cup squad. George."

***

George enjoys the odd diversion from talking about football and so it is when I speak to him for one of his Friday columns, which gives an insight into his life away from the pitch.

> *Looking at plans for my swimming pool helps take the cold edge off the winter. But guess what? I can't even swim! You may have seen pictures – of me on holiday in Majorca, sunning myself out at sea on one of those inflatable rafts. Now you know my little secret... I walked out to the raft!*
>
> *People may be surprised to hear that I'm not one of those guys who can power up and down a pool like Tarzan for hours on end but it's just one of those things.*
>
> *I played most games at school but when the other lads were learning to swim I was usually busy playing football. Then, when I was nine or 10, a friend of mine drowned while we were on holiday at Groomsport, Northern Ireland, and I became terrified of the water for years afterwards.*
>
> *I've managed to get over this fear. In fact I love the water now. As soon as my heated pool is ready, I intend to take lessons so that I can get as much fun out of taking a dip as my friends.*

George spends hours in and around the boutique. It is more than a business interest. Indeed, this year he came joint fifth in the Best Dressed Man in the World awards run by a magazine, tied with actor Robert Morley.

He is at this time a director of Lincroft Clothing Co Ltd, of Kennington Park Road, London, a firm specialising in modern fashions. Harold Tillman, a tall, angular man with a reputation for design, is the managing director of the firm, and with The Name geared to the merchandise, shares are doing well. Tillman is in Manchester and I ask him how he views George's future when he finished as a player.

"The way things are going he will spend his full time as a director of our company," he says. "And, make no mistake, George will make a good businessman."

Occasionally, a board meeting is held at "Che Sera" and George participates. But he has been known to stray away from the conference table and wander downstairs, leaving his co-directors to talk on between the "clunk" of snooker cue on ball.

Johnny Speight, writer-creator of outrageous, racist cockney television character Alf Garnett, throws a party in London. George is unable to attend because United have taken advantage of a break from routine with a trip to Jersey. So Johnny brings his party to George. To "Che Sera", anyway.

He calls George's house by telephone and records the whole show on the tape of George's answerphone system, so when George returns home from Jersey and switches on the system to see if there are any messages, he hears the blare of Johnny's festivities.

"Hello, George," says a man whose boozy breath almost creeps through into George's lounge. "I'm Sambuca." The more the tape winds on, the more inebriated Johnny's

guests become. "Georgie... ooh, Georgie," coos an ultra
feminine voice. "Give me a kish, Georgie", while a man
trips over himself pleading: "Georgie, Geor-gie! Please
sign this drink, Geor-gie."

George has a new regular girlfriend, Carolyn Moore, the 19-year-old Miss Great Britain from Nantwich, Cheshire. "You could say we're GB and Miss GB," he says. Carolyn is dark, with large brown eyes and a short, boyish hairstyle, and fits snugly into the image of George Best, Superstar. She smiles a lot and is friendly and is happy to serve up coffee and toast at "Che Sera" as well as sip champagne at a swank nightclub.

Life is good for the pop idols, and George is one of them. But he draws a bold line when it comes to the final push of youthful and misguided experience, the cliff edge of drug taking.

"I'm no angel, and I have never apologised for enjoying my life," he says. "My image is such that people tend to take me as a representative of my age group.

"My hair is long and I like what some people would call 'way out' gear. But my feelings against drug addiction are very strong. And not only because I am a professional footballer.

"My close circle of friends is made up of lads who feel just as strongly as I do, and they would never make athletes. Yet there have been times when we have been out together when people have actually boasted about drugs and taken for granted that I'm on them.

"Our answer is to end the conversation and part company with them. I have even come across well-known people who take drugs and say it's because they are bored. Bored! How on earth can they be bored when life is so good and they have all the money they can possibly need to get the most out of it?

"If I were not committed to training and playing regularly, I would be off to the airport at the slightest sign of depression, look at the departure schedule and take off. I can't understand why anyone in good health should be bored. There is so much in life to see, so much to do and, generally speaking, there are great opportunities for young people. What can they possibly gain from making monsters of themselves in dirty cellars?

"Occasionally, I treat myself to a big cigar. Perhaps once a month. But, like my friends, I don't touch cigarettes. Drugs are something else again. My friends and I have been horrified when people we have known have been missing for six months or a year and have suddenly turned up looking a wreck and talking madness, nonsense."

***

I arrange with Daily Express colleague James Lawton a "confrontation" between Manchester's two controversial football characters, George and City's assistant manager Malcolm Allison. George praised Allison in his column before the Manchester derby and indeed both have ghosted columns in the paper, so we invite them to lunch to talk over prospects before a local derby game. When I arrive at l'Auberge de France restaurant in Platt Lane, not far from City's ground, Malcolm is there, and we have a drink.

We talk about George, and a waiter comes to say there has been a telephone message to say he has been delayed.

"I can understand why George lets people down like he does," says Malcolm. "I sometimes have the same kind of trouble myself. You see, you get so many people talking to you during a day in our business that it's difficult to memorise everything, who said what, who you said you would meet and where, and so on. You get a sort of mental block at times."

George has one on this occasion. James arrives, and we decide that the three of us should start lunch because Malcolm has to go back to the ground to see his players. Eventually there is another telephone message. George can't make it after all. "Ah," says Malcolm. "He's scared!" * 10

A senior colleague at the Express is among those with no sympathy for George's excesses. He frowns when I argue that it is illogical to expect a person who is uniquely gifted, an artist in his sphere, to conform in every other respect. Frank Clough, of the Sun, who has had many dealings with George, disagrees. "George isn't complex," Frank says, "he the most uncomplicated bloke I know. His problem is that he's lost half a yard of pace".

Alan Ball, the England World Cup star and Everton captain, is transferred to Arsenal for £220,000. He is a friend of George's and, inevitably, when there is a big transfer fee there is speculation about George's worth on the open market. £500,000? George doubts it.

His Friday column appears in the paper on Christmas Eve and he tells me: "I can't see our clubs ever paying that much for somebody. If the Alan Ball deal doesn't set a limit for fees then I don't think it can be far off."

George is in a good mood. There is a party planned that evening at Che Sera.

He says: "I've got a couple of Christmas trees, one is inside and the other outside – for the goldfish. I expect I'll sleep most of tomorrow then go up to Mrs Fullaway's for dinner. Sunday means training again and then it's Coventry at Old Trafford on Monday. Back in the old routine – looking for two points at the top of the table."

There are mountains of festive cards from fans and wellwishers and we take a picture of George with them for our back page.

"I'd love to answer them all but I'd have no time for football," he jokes.

But away from the glitter and excitement of Christmas, I ask George a serious question.

Would he ever think of leaving Manchester United?

He says: "A tricky question, and the answer would depend on the situation. If, suddenly, the club began to struggle badly and I was offered the chance to move to a place where the chances of success were greater and the set-up better, I would have to consider it. Any player would.

"But if things were going well, as they are now, and I was told United were thinking of letting me go, I'd be sick."

PART TWO

THE DECLINE

"He was reckoned to be unfit for the match and so not allowed to take part. It is that rigour and discipline I want us to copy. For too often we come to Sunday worship spiritually untrained."

— Rev Michael Dunn, Vicar of St Justus, Rochester, Kent, urging parishioners to heed the Parable of George Best.

***

'Britain's swinging soccer star banished to tea and crumpets'

— New York Times headline

VI

A Man Must Fall
Seven Times

'Mrs Fullaway and Mr Fullavodka'

Winter and spring 1972

George admits that he is struggling for form and stories circulate that he is burning the candle at both ends and in the middle, even on nights before matches. "Rubbish!" he insists. "Some bastard has written to O'Farrell saying he's seen me in this place on such a night and that place the next night, and I'm at it on Friday nights. Rubbish! And I've told O'Farrell that. I never go out on Friday nights or before matches, but people are always seeing me! One time a long time ago I was dropping someone off somewhere in the car on a Friday night and had a bump. The story was that I was drunk and had a dozen girls with me. The truth was that I hadn't been out of the car."

Frank O'Farrell has called George a "model professional", a tribute to the player's willingness to work during training sessions. He has also added the caution: "George is full of good resolutions and good intentions, but he must learn that it is not enough to give them. You have to keep them."

George tells me he does not make resolutions. "I don't make them. So I can't break them." New Year 1972 dawns with dark clouds gathering over Old Trafford and "Che Sera".

United haven't won in four matches and their lead at the top of the First Division is cut to two points. George misses training for a week. Monday is a day off, Tuesday he does not feel up to putting in an appearance. By Wednesday it has become more difficult to go to The Cliff training headquarters, so he puts it off again. Thursday afternoon I go to the boutique to see him for his Express column. I am told he is at home. I telephone and Fred says George is in bed. There is nothing strange about that. He is often in bed on Thursday afternoons or early evening.

George comes to the telephone and we discuss ideas for the column. Express readers have unanimously voted him into their make-believe Great Britain team, so I ask George to name his list of players for such a representative side. He does and I write it.

Friday and the storm breaks with an announcement from Old Trafford that George has not trained all week and is dropped from the following day's home game against Wolverhampton Wanderers. I am as surprised as anyone. The world seems to be surrounding George's house when I arrive but I manage to get into the garage at "Che Sera" while Ken Stanley becomes a one-man relay team between George and gathering newspapermen. The paper is full of people wanting to have their say on the situation. A double spread is devoted to the fans' views with many supportive. George sees no one and later, when I manage to contact him by telephone, his only comment is: "I just can't say anything." He goes to Manchester Airport and, with Eddie Hindle, flies to London.

Speculation grows: he is to be married to Carolyn Moore; he wants a pay rise; he wants a transfer. George is followed to an Italian restaurant on London's Old Brompton Road where halfway through his meal he takes a call from a girl calling herself 'Carolyn'. They leave the restaurant in the early hours with friends in tow and head for a 'late night discotheque'. The girl's father, a plant-hire contractor, even issues a denial from his home in Wilmslow that his daughter is to marry Best. Carolyn arrives home on Saturday night before meeting up with George again at "Che Sera". The press follow the couple to a local railway station where George kisses Carolyn on the cheek before she takes a train back to London to continue work. Asked about a wedding, she says, "Marriage has never been suggested."

The only certainty is that O'Farrell is waiting to see him on the following Monday and is trying to come up with disciplinary action to fit the situation. O'Farrell has finally inherited the kind of problem that beset Sir Matt Busby: missed trains and the siege at the flat of actress Sinead Cusack during a stormy spell a year earlier.

Monday January 10

Newspapermen and television crews clutter Old Trafford's concrete forecourt like frustrated supporters looking for tickets for a big game. They are anxious for the arrival of the blue E-type Jaguar, but George turns up as a passenger in Eddie's Ford Capri and quickly disappears into the ground. Eventually we are summoned to hear O'Farrell's punishments for the prodigal: a fine of two weeks' wages (less than £400); extra training, mornings and afternoons with the junior players; no days off for five weeks; an order to leave "Che Sera" and go back to digs at Mrs Fullaway's. Mrs Fullaway, who was visiting relatives in Widnes when she heard the news, dashes back to her home in Aycliffe Avenue, Chorlton-cum-Hardy and prepares the twin-bedded room that George stayed in when he first arrived from Belfast.

A colleague turns to me and says, "Mrs Fullaway and Mr Fullavodka!"

O'Farrell has sampled what life can be like when George reacts instinctively to the combination of a series of irritating situations and, after bottling his feelings, suddenly explodes into rebellion. But O'Farrell tries to understand, and says: *"A man must fall seven times."*

Eric Todd, of The Guardian, whose long experience of Manchester football affairs has not dulled his wit, jokes: "Well, Frank, would you be good enough to ask George to call a press conference next time he has a mind to do something like this?"

George is at the boutique. He will not admit there was any one single reason for missing training, but confides: "I've worked hard for three years to get that house and I'm not leaving it now." His return to Mrs Fullaway's is a façade and it is an open secret that George is allowed to return to his home at United's discretion.

The Fifth Inn is not far from the boutique and George is lunching with Eddie and a business associate from Lincroft when I call to see how he has settled down again at the club. Great goals, memorable triumphs of skill over brawn and the spontaneous congratulations of team-mates are still fresh in mind from United's pre-Christmas surge of success.

I ask George how the other players took his return to the fold. He forks a piece of venison and says: "They've been great. All except one. I'm not saying who he is but his name is Bobby Charlton. Brian Kidd was great. He came back with me in the afternoon to keep me company when I was training with the youngsters. I really appreciated that."

***

Little more than a week after the showdown at Old Trafford, George electrifies the ground with a magnificent performance against Southampton. The match develops into the kind of situation United have experienced several times before: stalemate. This time their FA Cup hopes are in the balance in a third-round replay.

Southampton, with Mike Channon giving a superb hard-running, hard-tackling performance in midfield, are still in the game with more than a fighting chance. But George destroys them in extra-time with two goals scored with typical disregard for numerical superiority in the penalty area, and United win the tie 4-1.

Sitting next to me in the Old Trafford grandstand is Ken Stanley, and when George's second goal strikes home we rise instinctively with the rest of the crowd because the performance demands a standing ovation. Ken beams and punctuates his applause by saying: "They say he's lost a yard, but it doesn't look that way, does it? And if he has it's only fair to the others he plays against. Otherwise they'd have no chance at all!"

When George returns to the centre circle he turns towards the main stand and raises his arms in the air. It comes over even more clearly on millions of television sets as a double V-sign.

Why spoil such a triumph with a gesture like that? "I was doing it to the press," he tells me. "And I'm not apologising, because in similar circumstances I'd do the same again. I've told you before I don't care what they say about me. But they've been knocking my friends again. Calling them hangers on and a circus. And Mrs Fullaway's been getting obscene letters saying she's earning a fortune out of me.

"Some of them are really disgusting, and I've had enough of what the papers have been saying about everyone who associates with me. I didn't decide to do what I did on the spur of the moment. I'd had it in mind for a while. You can sense when you are going to have a fair game, and I sensed it last night. And I was ready to let the press know exactly what I thought about them."

VII

Best Wants To Leave United

*'I've got a story to tell... but I won't
tell it for nothing'*

George tells me he has received champagne and messages of support from Ringo Starr and Marc Bolan and asks if I can verify that the bubbly and best wishes really did come from them before he mentions it in his column. I ask the show business desk at the Express to check this for me and they call me back in the affirmative, adding, "Their representatives say they are surprised George didn't keep this to himself."

They are not the only stars that I come in to contact with through George. Muhammad Ali briefly comes into my life as a result of an unemployed labourer and former bare-knuckle boxer from Abingdon by the name of Paddy Monaghan who wants George to say a few words in praise of The Greatest for his fan club magazine.

Ali came into Paddy's life after being shown a petition signed by thousands of British people sent by Paddy to the boxing authorities in the United States in protest at the ban imposed on Ali because of his refusal to fight for his country in the Vietnam war.

So impressed was Ali that he sent Paddy airline tickets so that he could join him on a lecture tour of America. During the lectures Ali would call Paddy on stage, introducing him to the audience as, "My greatest fan." When Ali returned to boxing, Paddy had a place in his corner for one of his title fights. Some of Paddy's neighbours in Abingdon were sceptical about his association with Ali until the day *The Greatest* arrived on his doorstep.

Paddy stays at my home before meeting George and gives me Ali's New Jersey telephone number. He then calls him and introduces me to him. * 11

At one point in July, 1972, there seems to be a possibility of Paddy Monaghan working for Ali in Britain through George's agent, Ken Stanley. To that end I accompany Paddy and one of Ken Stanley's representatives to meet Ali in Dublin, where he is due to fight an American compatriot, Al "Blue" Lewis.

Ali, who has been out training, wears what look like diving boots. And sings me a rhyme after I ask him to say a few words into Paddy's cassette recorder for my two-year-old son Christopher:

> *Christopher who's only two*
> *This is Muhammad Ali speaking to you*
> *Don't be no fool*
> *Obey the rule*
> *And go to school*
> *Or I'll be after you*
> *When I've beaten "Blue"*

Later, when I attempt to replay the message, I realise I had failed to press the correct button and there was no recording. It is a huge disappointment.

***

Northern Ireland, exiled by the troubles at home, play Spain at Hull, and George is late joining the party, blaming problems with his car. Eddie is with him at the team headquarters in Scarborough.

February 16 and Northern Ireland draw the match 1-1. George mis-hits a free-kick into the Spanish penalty area, and Sammy Morgan, of Port Vale, celebrates his debut in the big time by being in position to take advantage and score the Irish goal.

That evening in Manchester, I see George in The Grapes. He is with Eddie and Malcolm Wagner. George treats me to a steak and Malcolm asks if it would be possible to get some film negatives for him of a picture taken some years earlier of George in the barber's shop, being shaved by Malcolm and an assistant in Edwardian dress. Malcolm wants to have the picture enlarged for a wall of an extension at his shop. We talk about the match. "A great free-kick, wasn't it?" jokes George.

"They kept you closely marked," I say.

"Yes," says George, "but Eddie and me had worked out some good Spanish swear words to use on that geezer who stuck close all the time."

"That Sammy," says Eddie, switching conversation to the young Manchester United forward Sammy McIlroy who, like Morgan, had made his first appearance for his country. "He kept hanging onto the ball trying to beat them himself instead of getting rid. He kept getting caught."

Eddie and Malcolm move away for a while and I talk to George about United, the way the swing has gone against them and his own form and future. "I'm sick," he confides.

How sick? Sick enough to ask for a transfer?

"Yes, sick enough to want to move." Why? Is it the club? Is it the manager?

"No, I've got nothing against the management. It's the team. It's just not good enough. It's just not going anywhere. I could go right through the team and find things wrong. People knock me when I'm not doing it, but when I'm not doing it who is? Brought along the right way, Sammy McIlroy could be a great player in five years.

But I can't wait five years for Sammy to become a great player."

Where would he go?

"Right now I'd go anywhere, anywhere I thought there could be success."

I ask George if he is prepared to allow his feelings to be published. "Yes, but I'm not going through all the aggravation it will cause for nothing. Ask them to make me an offer," he says.

How much?

"I'm not talking in figures. Let them make me an offer. I've got a story to tell, but I'm not doing it for nothing."

I leave The Grapes, filled with anticipation. What an exclusive story this promises to be...

I go back to the Daily Express in Great Ancoats Street, an impressive glass building. During a print run passers-by can see the printed pages as they roll off the rotary presses as if on a roller-coaster. In my mind's eye I can already see the George Best head-line on the page, about to cause a sensation.

Best wants to leave United!

After taking the lift to the editorial floor, I pass the bustling wire room, where copy is arriving from news agencies and via our London office, and stride excitedly past the sports sub-editors' desks and the clatter of the Remington typewriters on the news reporters' desks and in the copytakers' booths until I arrive at the editor's office. There I see the deputy northern editor, Ted Hodgson, acting editor on the night, and tell him what George has told me.

He says he does not like it. George Best is under contract to the Daily Express. Ted is clearly troubled. He does not want the news-paper to appear to be interfering in any dispute between George Best and Manchester United. Ted wants to know what sort of money George may be seeking.

I say I do not know.

"Thousands rather than hundreds?"

I say I would imagine so, but repeat that George simply asked for an offer to be made if we want his story.

Ted Hodgson calls me back into his office. He has contacted the editor. "He agrees with me. Tell George we're not prepared to pay for a story of this kind but remind him he is under contract to us."

As I prepare to leave, Ted says: "And if the story breaks, make sure we have it."

While understanding Ted's misgivings about running the story, I feel thoroughly disappointed. This is not just any leading player talking about asking for a transfer, it is George Best, the biggest name in the game, the player whose fame spreads far beyond the terraces.

VIII

Star Treatment

'Being a bit of a celebrity in my own way is
nothing compared to being George Best'

George is selecting models for a fashion show at Blinkers discotheque when I contact him to explain the situation.

Says George: "They won't offer me anything for the story but they say I'm not to let anyone else do it? Great! Anyway," he adds, "I've not decided what to do about it. I might see O'Farrell and make it a private matter or I might see him and make it public. I don't know which way I'll do it yet."

A few days later I see George again, this time accompanied by my sports editor, David Nicholls. The editor is wary of the situation and wants David to see what George is going to do. George says he is still undecided and is prepared to wait a while to see what develops. United are still involved in the FA Cup. There is still a chance they might end the season with success.

The season that began with such promise for United is crumbling week by week, game by game. A five-point lead at the top of the First Division is now a distant memory, difficult to believe, and the FA Cup run ends in defeat at Stoke. *12

George is thoroughly disenchanted, and when results go against United it becomes all the more difficult to combine his football with his pleasure. Mornings dawn on him like an intruder, and there are days when he misses training again.

Someone asks George how much of his ability to dazzle defenders was sheer skill and how much of it was hard work. He says: "If it happens in the first three minutes, it's skill. If it happens in the last three minutes, it's hard work!" Those last three minutes are growing longer and longer.

O'Farrell makes his first move into the transfer market in late February by signing the Aberdeen and Scotland defender Martin Buchan for £135,000, an acquisition that is to influence United's long term future but is unable to prevent the team's decline in the short term. George is at the Men's Wear Exhibition at Earls Court, London, where he bumps into Chelsea's brilliant midfield player Alan Hudson. He tells George that after coming up against the Scot in the recent Under-23 International, United have "bought a winner". Indeed, Buchan is an intelligent player and he eventually becomes United's captain, coordinating the defence as the team is revived under Tommy Docherty's stewardship. During one match Buchan clipped the United winger Gordon Hill round the ear. Quick witted, Buchan was once asked for a quick word by a radio reporter, and replied, "Velocity."

One morning a message is sent to United that George will not be reporting for training because he is feeling ill. Fred is tending a stretch of garden near the drive into "Che Sera" when a car he seems to recognise approaches.

"It was the club doctor," says Fred. "We know each other well, but this day he just strides on past me and up the steps to the front door. Olga answers it, but before she can say anything or do anything the doctor strides past her, too, and is inside the house. Straight away he says to Olga: 'Where's the bedroom?' She points and again before she can say or do anything he goes into the bedroom and closes the door. He's in there for a short time and when he leaves the house and gets into the car, I say: 'How is he, doctor?' He looks at me and says: 'Freddie (he always calls me

Freddie), you know how he is, Freddie', and off he goes. I gather he doesn't think there is much wrong with George."

O'Farrell has signed Ian Storey-Moore from Nottingham Forest, with the deal being clinched following an embarrassing weekend during which Derby County were the first to announce Moore's capture before Forest had completed the signing of the transfer forms. George takes the new boy out to dinner following a goalless draw with Everton at Old Trafford. "I thought he might be a bit lonely up in Manchester on his own, living in a hotel," George tells me. "Anyway, we had a good meal, a good chat and then he left early because he was training the following morning. I hope we get along as well on the field as we do off it." There is a brief period when Moore's arrival and his direct, flowing style rekindles George's own enthusiasm. But it does not last.

There is a new offer on the table to make a film, he tells me. He is keen to get involved, following in the footsteps of racing driver Jackie Stewart and French skier Jean-Claude Killy, who have recently made documentaries about their lives. "It will be in the style of the Beatles' Hard Day's Night or Help, the story written around my life as a modern day footballer," he says. George has come a long way from the days of watching Saturday matinees as a boy in Belfast.

***

Barry John is a king of the Welsh valleys, Cardiff Arms Park and rugby union; a fly-half of superb grace, bringing to the rugby grounds of the world the kind of magic George has brought to soccer. When they meet, at a Sportsman of the Year function, they find they have a great deal in common. They find communication easy, like exceptional painters who make contrasting patterns but have kindred talents.

Barry is on the verge of announcing his retirement, and is compiling an autobiography. He asks George to make a contribution and George invites him to "Che Sera" for a weekend. George shows Barry around Old Trafford and around his home, and they have a night out with friends. Enough for Barry to sample what life is like for the biggest name in soccer.

"You know, I suppose I get a bit of the star treatment where I come from," Barry tells me later. "Well, I thought I did. But being a bit of a celebrity in my own way is nothing compared to being George Best. I was only with him a couple of days, but even in that short time I saw the kind of pressures that surround George. They are really tremendous. Everyone wants to get close to him all the time. It must be terribly difficult for him."

Not everyone does get close to George, and even when they do, it is no guarantee that he will co-operate. "There was a time when I used to chase around everywhere. Not any more," he says. "I realised it was just impossible trying to go here, there and everywhere, so I stopped." But there is still that reluctance to say: "No."

Ivan Mauger is the world speedway champion and the king of Belle Vue, Manchester. He is opening a new speedway track at Barrow-in-Furness, Lancashire, and asks George to make a personal appearance. When the day arrives, Ivan calls at "Che Sera". George is not there. He waits, then goes to Manchester.

George is at the shop and tells Ivan he has to see a specialist about an injury. Ivan waits, worrying if he will make it to Barrow in time. George says he has to make a telephone call, goes back into the shop and slips out the back way. Ivan travels to Barrow alone to explain to the waiting crowd at the track that George will not be able to come after all.

There is talk of George being cited as a co-respondent in a divorce case, and when I ask him about it he nods and says it could happen. I ask if he is worried. "No, people seem to think you're a hero if you're in a divorce case these days," he says.

George complains to me that he is frustrated at "being on the outside looking in" as talk turns to who will win the silverware that season. United have long since slipped out of the title race and lose 3-1 to rivals Manchester City, who are competing for the championship with Leeds United, Liverpool and Derby County.

The public delivers a damning verdict after United slip to another defeat, this time a 3-0 reverse at Arsenal. Under the screaming headline 'SELL BEST SAY FANS', the supporters line up to vent their fury.

"United should sell Best — because he seems to have his mind too much on other things. He has too many business interests and doesn't show enough enthusiasm for football —and that is his real living."

— Anne Wolstenholme, 18-year old catering student, of Woodhouses, Failsworth, Lancashire.

"He's done too much, too soon. George Best isn't a team player and right now he doesn't appear to be interested enough in football. Of course United should sell him — but who's going to buy him ?"

— Arthur Scanlon, 47, parking meter warden, of Chorlton-on-Medlock, Manchester.

"He's too involved with things outside soccer. If United can get £350,000 for him, they should let him go. He'd play better for a London club."

— Malcolm Snyder, 28, tailor, of Bury.

"He's gone very quiet lately. If United are offered £150,000 for Best, they should sell. I've watched United for 50 years and they aren't the team they were."

> *— Fred Murphy, 78-year-old retired grocery manager, of Pendleton.*

"If I were George Best's mum I'd tell him to concentrate on playing football. He's a good player and I enjoy watching him on TV, but he doesn't seem to be helping United to do well. Yes, I think they should sell him."

> *— Mrs. Helen Cookson, 67-year-old grandmother, of Levenshulme, Manchester.*

But other fans are not so unforgiving...

"Manchester United must not sell George Best. They need him too much — but they should get rid of all the others. Then O'Farrell could go out and buy better players who are fit to play with Best. Everyone should leave him alone so he can get on with playing. People make too much fuss about his businesses and girlfriends"

> *— Barbara Silver, 21, secretary, of Prestwich*

"Best is too valuable and too good to sell—and United need him badly. Perhaps someone should stop him having so many outside interests."

> *— Gerald Stearman, 19, Sixth Former at De la Salle College from Unsworth, Whitefield.*

"I like George Best and I've got pictures of him. I want to be like him when I grow up. I like to play football."

— Jason Clarke, aged 3, of Shaw Heath. Stockport.

It seems that young and old from all walks of life are involved in the great George Best debate.

However, despite the fevered speculation that United might be tempted to transfer George, when his club season ends he is still in Manchester making tentative moves about his future.

Indeed, he seems in upbeat mood as he reveals his summer diary. He's off to Hamburg for Uwe Seeler's testimonial before a 10 day break "combining business with pleasure" in the Seychelles. Then it's back home for the Home Internationals with Northern Ireland before heading off to Israel and Greece with United and rounding it all off by "meeting up with a couple of my mates and heading off in the general direction of Majorca."

I pay him a visit at "Che Sera" on a Saturday before the British Championship international matches are played. He is alone when I call and goes into the kitchen to make tea. There is horse racing on the television in the fireplace and George asks me to keep an eye on a particular horse. "I'll bet it wins easy, and I haven't backed it," he says. "That's how it's been since I switched it on. I've been fancying horses, not bothered to have a bet, and they've all won!"

When tea is made and he emerges from the kitchen to join me at the round, white table, I ask if he has thought any more about asking for a transfer. "No, but I've been in to tell them what I want," he says. And what is that? "I've asked for £1,000 a week, and I also want the club to buy this house off me. I haven't been able to settle here at all."

And what is O'Farrell's reaction?

"He seemed to think it would be OK but said it would have to be put before the board, so I'll have to wait and see. Lincroft are doing well and I don't want to do anything that might upset things for them. I've an idea what I'll do if the club agrees to give me a rise and buys the house. We've thought of building a big place as near to the centre of Manchester as possible, and I'd have a penthouse on top with my own private lift and everything."

Having a ball:
Sunny Spain
beats the
Manchester rain

Life in the fast lane: George beside his beloved E-type Jaguar along with former girlfriend Eva Haraldsted

United expects: September, 1972

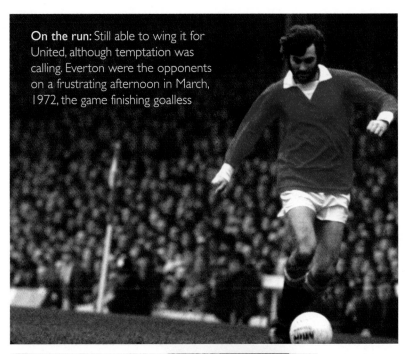

On the run: Still able to wing it for United, although temptation was calling. Everton were the opponents on a frustrating afternoon in March, 1972, the game finishing goalless

Belfast boy: This Is Your Life meant a family reunion in November, 1971, with mum Ann and dad Dick, pictured in earlier days with twin sisters Julie and Grace

Pride of Northern Ireland: George drew the crowds, although the political troubles brought problems. Inset left: Outside the team hotel on international duty. Inset right: An autograph for Northern Irish fans

Che Sera: Rare colour picture of the much talked about house, right

Blinkers United: Named after the nightclub, this charity ladies football team, consisted of girlfriend Eva Haraldsted, other players' partners and beauty contest winners

Summer's coming: With dreams of Wembley dashed and title hopes faded, perhaps the mind is drifting to Marbella during a break in training, April 1972

First plane anywhere: Flying out, October 1971

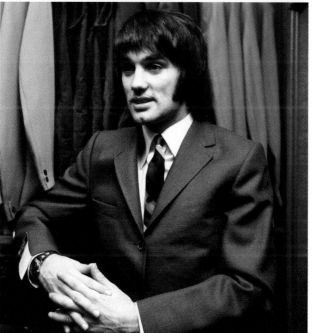

Birthday boy: Turning 26 in Marbella with friends and a press pack for company

Best dressed: When you've got your own boutique, you have to set the trends

The Georges: Not Marbella but Palma Nova, Majorca in June, 1969.
The girl is actress Susan George, who Best complained in his column
criticised him after their relationship had ended

IX

The First Plane Anywhere

'George has kicked the top off Ken's triangle'

George's dream has a short life. United go to Majorca for a quick break before flying on to play in Israel, but tell George he must stay behind and join the Northern Ireland squad for the international series. George goes his own way. He arrives home in the early hours of a May morning and decides he has had enough. He calls a taxi, goes to Manchester airport and asks for "the first plane anywhere". He ends up in southern Spain.

Friday May 19

Eddie Hindle is ready to join George in Marbella to find out what is going on. Eddie calls me at my office and asks if I fancy joining him. I say the office have already dispatched Stephen Harper, our man in Madrid. Eddie says he will keep in touch and calls me again from Heathrow airport, London, where he is awaiting departure to Spain.

"I've been thinking," says Eddie. "Everybody has a go at George as soon as something like this happens. They don't know why he's gone or anything, but immediately the knocking starts. They have a go at him about his football, about his nightlife, about his girls. About everything. And they just say: 'There goes that George Best, running away from everything again.' Don't they ever think that something might be wrong with George? That he might need help?" We talk until shortly before Eddie's flight is called.

Saturday May 20

George quits football, telling the world he has been drinking a bottle of spirits a day.

When a press colleague catches up with him, he is sitting in the lobby of a five-star hotel sipping a beer. He says: "People can think what they like. I have come here to relax for a few days." He talks openly about the reasons behind his drinking. "For two years, I have not been able to sleep properly. I have gone to bed at 2am and got up two hours later just to have a drink in the hope that it would get me off to sleep," he says. "It would take me nine months of very hard work to get even physically fit again. Now I am going away for six months – anywhere. I have finished completely with the Manchester scene." His plan is to "live off his investments" and turn his hand to business.

When the news reaches us I turn to my wife, Phyllis, and say: "George has just kicked the top off Ken's triangle." Two days later, George celebrates his 26th birthday with a posse of pressmen, Eddie and a cake.

Happy Birthday, Dear Georgie!

It had all the makings of a happy birthday, right enough. Sunshine. Champagne. A huge iced cake with twenty-six candles. There was a holidaymaker on one side and a business associate on the other to sing as George Best, Soccer's runaway star, celebrated his twenty-sixth birthday yesterday in Marbella, Spain.

There were greetings telegrams by the dozen. And there were smiles from George as he handed round the champagne. Yet somehow the sparkle was missing.

When a birthday phone call came from Miss Great Britain, Carolyn Moore, George wasn't up to take it.

A birthday message from the Northern Ireland team boss Terry Neill said simply that they would like him back in their team. "I appreciate the gesture," said Best.

"But my mind is made up about football. I'm sorry... but it's over."

There were no greetings at all from his mates at Manchester United. But he said: "I won't be going back to Old Trafford again."

The only word from the City of London was that shares in the company which bought his boutiques had dropped 7p on the Stock Exchange. Making the lad £900 poorer on the day. A costly sort of party, one way and another.

On the same day, the game that George failed to report for finishes Scotland 2, Northern Ireland 0 at Hampden Park in the British Home Championships. But a few days later, there is a famous victory at Wembley without George, Terry Neill scoring the only goal of the game.

Meanwhile, George tries to justify his absence by blaming United's trophyless season, saying that qualification for Europe might have made him stay for "one more year". He adds: "If I had my time again my country of choice wouldn't be England. When you talk to continental players about the number of games successful teams in England have to play they think you're joking. We're the laughing stock of Europe".

Away from the sports pages, life chugs along as normal back home. Friday nights on BBC and as well as Mike Yarwood, It's A

Knockout and the compulsory Western, George's 10-minute skills programme is on TV after the six o'clock news. So, on Friday, May 24, 1972, while our hero is relaxing in Marbella, the nation's youngsters are watching him explain the intricacies of the reverse pass.

***

Several rooms link together to make the Ken Stanley Organisation at the top of the stairs of St George's House, Huddersfield.

The reception room is small and neat and filled with pictorial reminders of the top sports personalities associated with the business. It is easy to pick out George, Denis Law and the England World Cup squads: glory at Wembley and the broken dream of Mexico. On one side is the boardroom with a door leading off into a sizeable storeroom.

This is for sample sports bags, plastic footballs, games and the like, but the Organisation has extensive warehouse facilities elsewhere. To the other side of reception is the general office where Ken's daughter, Sue, busies herself alongside friendly office girls Trish and Myra. There are lots of birthday cards for George, sent from all parts of the country. Some are large, some are small. Some elaborate, some simple.

Through another door is a fair-sized room usually occupied by Ken's son, David, and this leads to John Lamb's compact office. Finally, there is Ken's hive, smart and businesslike, with files and folders, and "in" and "out" trays piled high with work.

Sounds from outside rise up to suggest all is normal; business as usual at the railway station across the noisy one-way street filled with traffic moving into the square.

Ken sits behind his desk, oblivious to sounds outside the office, besieged by incessantly ringing telephones. He is trying to steady his empire and is coping with admirable calm and efficiency. He smokes a pipe and gently rat-tat-tat-tats his desk with fingers that betray a little of the strain he is under.

The calls keep coming.

> *"Is it right?"*
> *"Has he really finished?"*
> *"Won't he play again?" ask anxious manufacturers.*

Contracts, from English plastic footballs to an American goods chain, hang in the balance. Ken reassures people as best he can. He tells them he will soon be going to Spain to see George and is sure the position will be resolved satisfactorily. It is a time for patience.

"Why does he do things this way?" asks Ken, shaking his head and answering his own question with his own thoughts.

"I've told him so many times: 'Look, George, if you are ever in any difficulty of any kind, if you ever need any help or advice, all you have to do is pick up a phone and call me or send a telegram. I'll be on my way to see you straight away. Japan. Anywhere in the world. You just have to call.'

"But no. He goes away like this. People are being very good about it. They are prepared to wait for a while for things to cool a little and to give me time to sort things out. But why does he do things this way?"

I have come to know Ken quite well from my dealings with George, including editing his club magazine, a quarterly publication for club members that has tended recently to open with the words: "Well, in trouble again…"

The phones in Ken's office rest long enough for him to reflect: "I've told George we can conquer the world together and if he wants to we still can. All the way down the line we've done everything to make sure he will be secure financially. I've been looking forward to the day when I can say: 'Right, George, here's your million.' But he goes his own way and does things like this. I've got other clients to think about, too. We have so much work on without this happening. The World Cup, for instance. Which reminds me…"

Ken puts through a telephone call to the England team manager Sir Alf Ramsey to confirm that he will be able to see him at Hendon Hall Hotel, the England team's quarters in London, that evening. Towards the end of their conversation, George's name crops up and Ken explains briefly how the situation has affected him. When Ken replaces the receiver, I ask what Sir Alf had said about George. "He just said: 'You've got to have respect,'" says Ken.

In Marbella, George is still watched by newspapermen. Ken arrives. So, too, does Malcolm Wagner, and they spend some time relaxing at Australian Lew Hoad's tennis ranch. Manchester United are in Majorca, preparing to go on to Tel Aviv.

There are still hopes that George will join them and talk the situation over. There are rumours that Sir Matt Busby has been in touch to set up a private meeting, which he denies to the press. Frank O'Farrell plays it cool, saying he will not "prejudge" Best.

George stays on the mainland despite efforts to bring about a reconciliation.

The days laze by until George decides to return to Manchester for a brief "hello" before leaving for Majorca and his summer holidays.

George, Eddie and Malcolm arrive at Heathrow airport and catch another flight to Manchester, where photographers and television crews are waiting again.

George and his friends go first to "Che Sera" for a meal, then on to The Grapes and Annabell's.

Life is pretty much the same for George Best, ex-footballer.

While at The Grapes, I tell Eddie Hindle that George has made the situation difficult.

"You're saying he's let you and the Express down?" Eddie responds.

"Letting you down is nothing. What about United and George's sponsors? You've no idea."

PART THREE

THE LIMBO

"The Best is the
enemy of the good."

*— Title of a motion put down on the
Order Paper in the House of Commons
on May 24 1972,
by Mr Michael Clark Hutchison
(Tory, Edinburgh South).*

"The Speaker, Mr Selwyn Lloyd,
should "censor" the motion.
Many of us have our own views
about George Best, but this is a
calculated insult to a young man
who cannot answer back. Whatever
he has done, or not done, I feel
that this is a matter for his
own club, for himself and for
Sir Matt Busby".
*— Mr James Johnson
(Labour, Kingston Upon Hull West)*

"May I congratulate you
and thank you."
*— Sir Robert Cary
(Tory, Withington, Manchester)*

X

Travelling Companion

Summer 1972

It is 10 days since George blew out the candles on his birthday cake and, apparently, his career. Thursday, June 1, is a busy day. The office wants me to accompany George to Majorca the following day, when he starts his annual sojourn, but before there is time to pack even a change of socks I get word that the situation has been resolved behind the scenes. George is making a "comeback". I write a piece and trace George to the opening of Simm's, a restaurant club in Manchester, and ask him to confirm the story. He reads my copy and says: "It's right. But no quotes. Frank O'Farrell would kill me." Officially, there is no confirmation.

I go to the Express office to collect a cash advance on expenses for the trip and discover that my story, filed as a straight forward report that George has seen O'Farrell to patch things up with United, has been re-written in an airy-fairy style by Ted Hodgson.

The vandalised version, with my name on it, includes the following:

> *"If Best does not report for training as usual with his team-mates at the end of July, I will eat colleague*

Desmond Hackett's brown bowler hat – if there's any left!"

London office apparently took one look at the re-write and asked, "Is there a story, or is there not?"

Ted, unabashed, invites me to accompany him for a drink with a couple of colleagues. A couple of hours later, wary of my flight in the morning, I call the office and ask them to arrange for a taxi to take me home.

Time drags on and eventually I call the office again to be told a taxi had been sent 40 minutes ago. "It hasn't arrived," I said. "I'm waiting here in the Beethoven Club now." Overhearing this, a waiter taps me on the shoulder and says, "Rembrandt Club." A second taxi is sent for me.

Next day, on schedule, another taxi drops me off at Manchester Airport, stopping behind Fred's estate car.

He has given George a lift and is on his way back to "Che Sera". George is in the lounge upstairs and there are a few reporters and photographers. At Heathrow George faces a battery of cameras and is asked over and over: "Is it right you're coming back?" He just says: "I can't say anything." As we walk up the corridor towards the transfer passengers area I show him a copy of Time, the American news magazine, which has devoted a whole page to his recent escapades. He seems impressed.

Eddie Hindle and a business associate from Lincroft are at Heathrow to meet George and he says he is spending the afternoon in the city before catching a late afternoon flight to Palma.

They invite me to join them for lunch and we leave the airport in the comfort of an American car driven by the man from Lincroft. Eventually we arrive at the Old Brompton Road, and Franco Restaurant. The man from Lincroft says he will see us later and leaves George, Eddie and myself outside the restaurant. When

George enters he is greeted like a lost son by the friendly Italians who own the place. We are ushered to a table beside a large palm tree that disappears through the roof, part of which is glass and slides back on days like this when the sky is blue and the sun can make you feel like a Caesar.

I take a seat facing George and Eddie at our round table, and to my left and their right an Italian wedding lunch is in full swing, with rows of guests each side of a long table bringing the room to life with their happy talk and unbridled laughter. When soup arrives George tastes it then calls back the young waiter and tells him it is not as hot as it might be. "Gazpacho," George chides him gently and goodnaturedly, and the young man smiles.

The food is superb and as we eat Eddie says: "Simple but brilliant. That's the food here. And they all come here, you know. All the top people. Lord Snowdon and all those people."

George interjects: "He's here now", and Eddie and I laugh. "He is," George insists. "Behind you. But don't turn round and look." I laugh again, determined not to fall for the joke. But George nods to affirm his words, and Eddie nods, too.

I cannot resist the temptation, and glance over my shoulder swiftly. Lord Snowdon is sharing a table with friends and wearing a green bush shirt gathered by a wide leather belt, and grey trousers. An urban, clean-shaven Dr Livingstone.

Lord Snowdon and his party decide to leave before we have completed our meal and their journey takes them through a narrow pass between George and the backs of chairs belonging to the wedding guests.

As Lord Snowdon approaches this exit, he pauses and glances down towards George, then squeezes on through. When they have gone, George looks up and smiles mischievously.

Coffee and a few sambucas later, we take a taxi to the Lincroft factory in Kennington Park Road, where director George talks business and Eddie picks up some samples to take back to the north. Harold Tillman then drives us back to Heathrow for the service flight to Palma.

As we await boarding and stand in the small departure lounge, each with a seat number affixed to our ticket, curious eyes sneak darting glances at George. His fellow passengers behave almost shyly towards him, even the one or two who step forward to ask for autographs.

Once inside the aircraft, George takes a seat next to the window and almost immediately falls asleep.

Our neighbours on the flight take a keen interest in the slumbering VIP and seem to regard me as (a) an undersized, cut-price bodyguard; (b) his agent; (c) a relative or friend.

An elderly lady travelling with her husband looks across at George for a while and, careful not to awaken him, mouths a silent

I-S-H-E-A-L-L-R-I-G-H-T-?

across the gangway for me to lip-read, and I assure her he is, with due solemnity. The captain taps me on the shoulder and asks if George would mind signing a couple of autographs for his children. When he awakens, of course. I say I am sure he would not mind.

George opens his eyes as soon as the plane touches down at Palma and I tell him he is a wonderful travelling companion. He smiles and says: "I always sleep on planes. In fact, when United played Estudiantes in the World Club Championship I slept all the way back from the Argentine to England."

During summer and late autumn days Palma Airport is an anthill of human holiday traffic, and it is pleasant on this particular Friday evening to pass through in relative quiet and without the hustle, bustle and time-lag of peak-period baggage transit. I glance behind

Seeing red: Consoled by Tony Dunne and Bobby Charlton after being sent off for United

Reunion: David Sadler does the talking at training in July, 1972 as George, Alex Stepney and Pat Crerand listen

Away from it all:
Alone with his thoughts

Postcard from Spain:
George's fanclub
newsletter explaining
more about the events
of summer, 1972

Regular haunt: At the end of the bar, left, sipping a beer in the Gomila Grill, Palma. Above: John Roberts chats with Pat Crerand and Sir Matt Busby

Blowing his future: A picture of George's 26th birthday cake in Marbella that would appear in newspapers the world over

If you can't stand the heat…
Taking it easy, relaxing by the pool in Marbella

Downtime: A busy bar, full of swirling smoke and conversation with friendly faces – an evening at Slack Alice's, George's new nightclub

Roll with it: Turning up for training in his leased white Rolls Royce, December 1972, although the season would soon be over for George

Playtime: A spot of tennis to pass the day at Lew Hoad's ranch – in between lazing on the beach

Centre of attention: George enjoys some female company

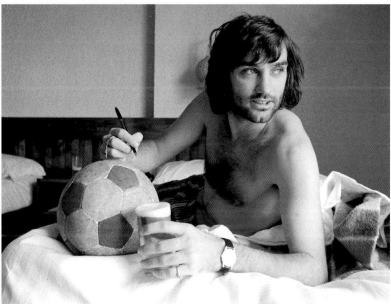

Room with a view: On a high in a Marbella hotel but still time to sign a ball

L47G6

L49G6

New admirers:
Surrounded by
children in
Majorca as he
puts on his boots
and United shirt
for the 'comeback'
and then ...
all alone to
contemplate what
the future holds

and see that George has travelled as far as customs control, where a zealous officer has singled out his luggage for scrutiny. A couple from the London flight jokingly castigate the officer, saying: "Don't you know who this is? George! George Best!"

Soon George emerges and is met by a friend, George Harrison ("no, not the 'My Sweet Lord' George Harrison. I'm another") from London.

And so begins his 35-day retreat to the sun.

XI

International Playboys

*'I believe it is within a man himself
to shape his life'*

This is my fourth visit to Majorca. The previous three times were for holidays in 1963, 1965 and 1970. On each occasion I noticed how much development had taken place, how many new hotels and bars had sprung up. In 1963, for example, Palma Nova and Magaluf were relatively quiet beach resorts. Now they are bustling by day and night.

Tim Brown, a freelance journalist based in Madrid, is at the Hotel Melia Mallorca, on the bay of Palma, and we talk about the events at Marbella.

"I remember the Sunday, when George held his press conference and told all the reporters why he was quitting," says Tim. "It was a moving occasion and when all the questions had been asked and were answered there was a feeling of sadness. Reporters went up to George and shook his hand and said things like: 'I'm sorry this has had to happen but thanks for everything, George.' But what do you think? The very next day two of these blokes approached two girls who were supposed to have been with George, asked them if they thought he was any good in bed and were going to write what they said. Imagine that! The very next day!

"Another time George was sitting in a bar and there were some Americans in the place. One of them put on a sarcastic voice and shouted: 'Georgie! Georgie! Georgie! Who IS this Georgie?' George got up, went over to where they were and said: 'Look, I don't mind you talking about me, but not while I'm here.' They shut up, quickly."

Later, George tells me about a journalist he calls "the man with the size nine ears". Says George: "No matter where I seemed to go in Marbella, as soon as I started a conversation with someone I could sense this geezer nearby and, sure enough, he'd be pretty close, straining his ears to catch what was being said."

I accompany George and George Harrison to the bar and they are talking with a couple of Englishmen when one of them punches George Harrison, seemingly without provocation. The two Georges leave and I continue talking to the older of the two men, unable to make sense of what has taken place. "So, you're from the Express, are you? Well I know your sports editor in London, Ken Lawrence," he says cryptically.

Next day when I visit George, I start talking about the incident in the bar. "Why don't you tell the whole beach, John!" he snaps.

Malcolm Wagner also arrives to join George Harrison and George, and most days they can be found around Bar Sol beach, Palma Nova. Siv, a slimly beautiful Swedish nurse, is usually in their company, but there are always girls within range.

George's sunbathing is punctuated by endless requests for pictures by holidaymakers with their Instamatic cameras, and often at around four o'clock in the afternoons the group leave Bar Sol to play tennis. Most evenings follow a pattern, starting with drinks and dinner at the Gomila Grill, near Tito's nightclub in the discotheque belt of Palma.

The Gomila, eye-catchingly neat with a bright white façade dominated by a large circular window, is managed by Felix, from Barcelona, a jovial, busy man who used to work at a hotel in Manchester and is married to an English girl. From the Gomila,

George and his party often move on to Tiffany's discotheque, about 300 yards away.

Particularly partial to Scandinavian girls seeking sun and fun like himself, George, as ever, is never short of short-term companions and one-night stands during his annual breaks in Majorca. It will be remembered that one of his most publicised liaisons was with Eva Haraldsted, who asked for George's autograph during United's tour of Denmark in 1969 and ended up living with him in Manchester.

There was talk of marriage until George told a female journalist he slept with that he might change his mind. The journalist wrote the story, Eva was furious and, although George insisted they were not engaged, she sued him for breach of promise and was paid £500.

George is always the centre of attraction at Bar Sol and continually meets old acquaintances from previous visits. Malcolm stretches out on a beach chair, rests a floppy hat over his eyes as a shield against the sun and says: "We're all IPs." What, I ask, are IPs?" He smiles and says: "International Playboys!"

Malcolm does not need his hat as a sun shield on the Monday following George's arrival. Rain contrives to make the Bar Sol beach look like any English resort and George, George Harrison, Malcolm and Siv stay in the bar. The two Georges and Malcolm play cards and I decline an invitation to join them. I sit and watch. George looks out at the rain and says: "Look at it. I've known it go on like that for a week here." George asks George Harrison about a card. "It was 'arts," says Harrison, and George mimics the Cockney accent, repeating: "Arts? Arts? Hearts, George, hearts!" The banter continues and twice during a hand Malcolm plays a wrong card. "Malcolm," says George, "you're making more mistakes than Bobby Charlton!"

The weather brightens, but it is difficult to look at George, still caught in his personal storm, without wondering what the future will bring. I think of other great players who have clung to their careers as long as time would allow and have felt lost when the game has gone on without them. It was this withdrawal symptom that prompted Raich Carter to say: *"Old footballers should be shot."* George is not an old footballer, yet here he is playing the role of a drop-out. I reflect that it is only months since Manchester United were England's number one club and George talked to me about the player he idolised.

"I keep hearing that I've not been involved personally in every minute of every game," he began. "This is true, because I am playing as a striker. I am on the field mainly to score goals. And my style has always been to work with the ball rather than control the flow of play. Before I finish I would love to attempt the style of one of the greatest players of all time; the player who was my biggest inspiration. Alfredo di Stefano. He could do it all and, during the course of a game, would appear just about everywhere, starting a move in one half of the field and finishing it with a shot or a header at the other end. A manipulator.

"When I was a boy kicking a ball in the streets of Belfast I had no great idols. My favourite team was Wolves, because it was around the time of their great games against the continentals, and my friends and I used to play 'Wolves v Spurs' and there would usually be a big race to be first to say 'I'll be Danny Blanchflower'. It was not at this time that Di Stefano made such an impact on my career, even though he was the big name in Europe.

"I came to realise his greatness later, when I became a professional. I began to take a big interest in him during my early years at Old Trafford. I've spent hours watching a film of that 1960 European Cup final at Hampden Park, when Real Madrid beat Eintracht 7-3. I still have the film in the room Mrs Fullaway keeps for me. Whenever I think of that game I can see Di Stefano, in his own half, sending Gento away for a raid down the wing, then suddenly arriving in the penalty box to score. He was that kind of player. If he took a corner kick, you expected him to dash into the goalmouth and put the ball into the net."

When he retired, Di Stefano said he felt George would succeed him as football's top man in an inside-forward position. I think of this as I look at George at Bar Sol. Di Stefano, who adopted Spain after being transferred from the Argentine, is just across the Mediterranean, manager of the Valencia club. I decide to contact him and, with the help of an interpreter, ask for his views on George.

Di Stefano says: "I admire George Best very much. I do not want to say anything about his private life because I do not know about it. He is surrounded by pressures of all kinds, and these are his greatest problem. Perhaps he believes now that he is phenomenal, that he does not need to take special care to look after himself. If that is so, then he is wrong. Perhaps now, while he is still young and strong, he can do this, but he must think of the time when life may catch up with him. His health can take a lot now, but he must be careful for the future.

"I am a married man with five children, but I do not believe the situation of a man, whether he is married or single, means very much. There are many single men who lead normal, interesting lives without excesses. And there are also many married men who are just the opposite, completely unfaithful.

"I believe it is within a man himself to shape his life the way that suits him best. As for the mental state of George Best, I believe what he needs is a good advisor, someone close to him who can help to guide him, show him the right way. He must decide for himself what he is doing now and in the future. Is it business or is it football? It amuses me when people ask if I would like George to play for Valencia. Of course! For us it would be wonderful to have such a player, but we do not have enough money to buy him and there would never be the chance. It will never be possible. We could perhaps arrange his mind, but not his bank account! George Best is a great player. It is too astonishing for me to even think he will be lost to the game."

In return for translating Di Stefano's comments, the Melia's PR asks if I will agree to being interviewed by a local newspaper, which subsequently runs a feature about the "loquacious" John Roberts, "Best's shadow".

George turns so that his back is exposed to the sun and asks me: "Why did they send you? Do they think I'm getting married?"

I say I do not know why exactly but presume it is in case there is a development.

Ajax have won the European Cup for the second successive season, beating Inter Milan 2-0. "George likes the Cruyff kid," says Malcolm. "He's a good player," says George, "and he's in a good side, isn't he?" George looks around and says: "Let's do something flash." He calls to one of the waiters and orders two bottles of champagne and some orange juice. "We're having Buck's Fizz," says Malcolm.

"The orange takes a bit of the tang out of the champagne. It's how the Regency Bucks used to drink it."

Bottles of Heineken are more familiar among the beach boys, although vodka is George's favourite, which makes me wonder why, in the story that George has quit football, it was claimed he drinks a bottle of whisky a day.

In my experience (although not privy to his lifestyle 24 hours per day), George is not a fill-up, fall-down drunk. My guess is that the effect on his system is steady and cumulative.

XII

The Comeback

'There's no glory now...'

Bar Sol beach has its own self-styled "guru", an Englishman called David who practises yoga on the sand between earning his living as a masseur. His table and other equipment pack away into a compact, portable box, so David is ready to work within seconds of arriving at the beach.

He is always in demand and appears in almost as many tourist snapshots as George as he ties his body into knots. He is one of the characters of Palma Nova and his skilful fingers help to keep George in reasonable shape.

Ken Stanley telephones me at the Hotel Melia and asks me to pass a message on to George that Frank O'Farrell would like to hear from him.

George and Malcolm are lunching outside Bar Sol when I arrive, and George says he will telephone O'Farrell later from Palma. I contact O'Farrell who tells me it is now in order for George to confirm that he would like to play for United again and that the club will make a statement the following day.

I see George at the Gomila Grill in the evening. He is with Malcolm and has not telephoned O'Farrell.

I tell George what O'Farrell has said and he dictates a statement for publication, the gist of which is:

"A short time ago I went away
to make a decision and now I realise it was
the wrong decision.
I would like to go back and play for
Manchester United."

Malcolm suggests George telephones O'Farrell from a nearby hotel. George wavers momentarily and I say I had better go back to the Hotel Melia to file copy. I speak to O'Farrell and tell him George will be in touch later. When I return to the Gomila, George is talking with Malcolm. Shortly afterwards George leaves and Malcolm and I order spaghetti bolognese. We eat, drink and talk.

"I was with George when he went to see O'Farrell before we came here," says Malcolm. "When he came out and got in the car he didn't say anything and we drove off. He still didn't say anything, so I said: 'Well?' and he said: 'Well what?' I said: 'Well, what happened?' And he said: 'Oh, he talked about wolves.' So I said: 'Wolves? Wolves?' wondering if there was going to be a transfer or something, and he said: 'Yes. You know, about the boy who cried wolf.'"

Malcolm tells me how he used to play in a pop group called The Whirlwinds that evolved in to 10cc and how George helped him out when he first went into business as a hairdresser, and we talk about how life has affected George. Eventually George returns for a moment, looks at Malcolm and me, winks at Felix and says: "Oh, I can see I've been getting some stick from those two!"

Manchester United confirm that George has been in touch with them and say they will discuss the future with him when he returns from holiday. With this development, I return to Manchester.

Uncertain how long I would have to stay in Majorca, I asked an artist at the Melia to draw a portrait of my infant son, Christopher, from a photograph. He makes a splendid job of this and presents it to me framed. After boarding the flight to Manchester , I go to my window seat and jam the frame in the curve of the fuselage. On arrival, the rest of the passengers disembark while I remain, struggling to dislodge the frame. * 13

Express photographer Peter Jackson and I are sent to cover the story of George's return home, and Peter hopes to persuade him to pose for a particular picture before he leaves. George took to Majorca his United training kit and boots, and Peter asks him to wear them for a picture illustrating the "comeback".

George is still at Bar Sol beach with the "IPs". Malcolm and I look out over the Mediterranean and he says: "People say we just hang around George for the glory, but there's no glory now. Just the nasty cracks about being hangers on." Eventually, George agrees to pose for the pictures. It is late afternoon when he emerges from apartment 5c, Eden Rock, overlooking the bay of Magaluf.

As children look on, Peter takes his shots from all angles as George goes through a series of exercises near a swimming pool outside the apartment block. Afterwards I want to interview him but he says he is tired and just wants to sleep. His mood is black. We go back into the apartment block, along a concrete corridor to an elevator. As George presses the elevator button, I ask: "Are you worried about the reaction you will get from the crowd at Old Trafford?"

He shakes his head and says: "Not at all."

We reach George's apartment and he says: "Right, I'm going for a kip."

I say: "Look, I won't keep you two minutes. Just a few words."

He begins to lose patience and snaps: "I'll only repeat the rubbish I told you before."

We go inside, where I try to reason with him and say: "Look, you've let a lot of people down. You can't just go back and pretend nothing has happened. For your own sake."

He just strolls about the room and says: "I just want to go back and play as I can." I leave it at that.

Peter is anxious to get his film to the airport. The Express has told him to put the film on a Manchester flight, so off he goes. He returns to the hotel white faced and in an agitated state. "I've posted them," he groans. "I've posted the photographs."

I order a drink to settle his nerves and ask him to explain what he is talking about. "I asked at the airport where I should leave the package for the Manchester flight and I was directed to a box in a wall. I've posted them!" We adjourn to a bar but Peter is inconsolable and dreads calling the office.

Next day, when he can no longer delay contacting the Express, he walks to his room like a condemned man, only to emerge punching the air like George after scoring a goal against Benfica and shouting in triumph: "They've got them! I didn't post them! What the man at the airport told me to do with the package was right after all!" This calls for more drinks, consumed this time with smiles.

Back at home, I hear that there are complaints about George from some team-mates. Bobby Charlton is caught by press at Heathrow Airport. He says: "If it wasn't for him we wouldn't be going on holiday to Bermuda. It's impossible to go anywhere in Europe because you get pounded by British tourists asking what's happening to George Best." His wife Norma adds: "All the people connected with George have their phones ringing perpetually. Why doesn't George face the publicity himself?"

As George's holiday nears its close and the harsh realities of renewed pressures in Manchester threaten like the first chill of winter, he makes the most of his time left on the beach and in the sun. He indulges in games that add to the carefree atmosphere at Bar Sol. "Guru" David attracts a crowd of spectators from their sun beds when he builds an awesome test of karate skill with wood and bricks, and retires to "meditate". Each time he appears to study the target the crowd becomes larger.

He meditates, meditates and meditates, until the spectators realise that the joke is on them and that he has no intention of performing the deed.

George introduces a game with empty bottles, spacing them evenly in line, then blindfolding a friend, Mike, a strong, stocky blond from Switzerland, whose task is to walk the line without touching the bottles. Each successful step is greeted with applause. Then George sneaks in and picks up the remaining bottles, leaving the contestant to step high over imaginary obstacles while the spectators continue to cheer each move.

Somebody arrives with a plastic football and we have a kick-about. George is disgusted – I'd like to say surprised – at my lack of ball control. I should have stuck with the table football game we played earlier.

July 7

The exile is over. Friends gather at the check-in point at Palma airport to say farewell, and when George and Malcolm arrive they manage to get permission for the group of well wishers who have shared the holiday to join them in the lounge through passport control for a farewell drink. Malcolm buys a round and we all say "cheers!", though our group is international. Eventually we are called to the departure gate. All the other passengers to London are aboard when we reach the aircraft.

George and Malcolm are booked on a flight from Heathrow to Manchester. Peter[*14] and I try our luck on stand-by tickets and are successful. Eddie Hindle is at Manchester airport, where pressmen crowd in again to remind George that the party is over.

Shortly after George's return, the Express send me to London to make a statement to their solicitor. Concerned that George's Sunday Mirror interview has compromised his contract with the Express, the solicitor asks me to detail the events leading up to his absconding to Marbella. I stress that George gave the Express the option of buying the story concerning his disillusionment with United.

Having taken notes, the solicitor says, "We'll change the colloquialisms and then you can sign the document."

My overriding impression is that there is a perception that I have begun to empathise with George too closely.

TALK OF THE TOWN

Special assignment! Shadowing Best

by HAROLD J. GREENBERG

John Roberts, Daily Express sports columnist.

AT THE Hotel Meliá Mallorca is John Roberts, a Daily Express journalist, who has been sent here especially to be the 'shadow' of George Best during his stay here.

Like most sports reporters, he is friendly and extremely loquacious.

«Usually, I am a sports columnist specialising in football. But now I have been asked to be George Best's 'shadow'. My newspaper, the Daily Express, has the world's exclusive right on the Manchester United player.»

—Didn't the Daily Mirror have the exclusive rights to George Best?

«There was some confusion about this, and the Mirror took advantage of it.

«There is now a lawsuit going on in England about this. It is a very delicate and dangerous thing.

«Best has gone through a great crisis, and it is possible that he may have more problems.»

—Is there another English journalist here like yourself with an identical mission?

«No, I am the only one. I am accompanied only by a photographer of the Express.»

—What does Best receive for this exclusive with you?

«Too much! More than they pay me!» he laughed.

«George Best has been talked about a lot — about his character, private life, and so on. What are the facts?

«Since he was 17, George hasn't had a private life, or been able to be a normal person.

«He is always surrounded by people. There is always a camera close by. His life is known minute to minute.

«Is it partly understandable, since Best earns enormous sums.

«Sometimes what happens ... he ... he will go out to a show, and then he becomes the show! On many occasions, I accompany him, and can tell you that this is a tremendously disturbing thing.

«And sometimes he does stupid things and doesn't know how to give reasonable answers at the time.

«He is not organised, nor careful, in his business engagements, and he often arrive late.

«But he doesn't have problems with women, because they always wait for him.»

—And his character?

«He is happy and very friendly to those who are really sincere with him.

«He is troubled by the bad propaganda about himself in the past, and the bad propaganda which continues.

«He doesn't want to be a product of publicity, but he also cannot stop being a product of his own fame.

«Where he wishes, he is intelligent. His column in our newspaper is worthy of a professional, and it is one of the most widely read in England.»

—What about George Best's future?

«After this vacation, which is his preparation for the next season, he wants to show, for a year at least, that he is the best football player in Europe.

«Later, it is possible that he will live temporarily in Majorca. Here he has his own life and he can count on real friends.».

—When is he returning to England?

«He is leaving for London on Sunday.»

Majorca Daily Bulletin, July, 1972

PART FOUR

THE FALL

'You've had some problems, but we all have these upsets, George. You must always try to overcome them as best you can because if you miss training you won't be gaining, George'

— *Message from Muhammad Ali*

'When I look at myself I don't see the man I wanted to be'

— *Bruce Springsteen,*
One Step Up (Tunnel Of Love)

XIII

Going His Own Way

'He is looking for something.
Something that isn't there...'

Manchester United suspend George for two weeks for his breach of contract and the Marbella affair, and order him to go into lodgings with Pat Crerand, once a team-mate, now the club's youth coach. "They've clipped his little finger again," one United player says in response to the punishment. The arrangement is that George will stay with Pat and wife Noreen in their four-bedroomed house in Sale. "I won't be a sergeant major, we'll be buddies," announces Crerand to the press. "I like Paddy. He won't be a nursemaid," says George. "I can still come and go as I please. It's just a matter of him ensuring regular hours and regular food." Also in the house will be one of George's biggest fans – eight-year-old Patrick Crerand, along with six-year-old Lorraine and three-year-old Danny. But the arrangement does not last long and soon, as negotiations go through for the sale of "Che Sera" to 26-year-old self-made millionaire Irishman Paddy O'Dwyer for £40,000, George moves back to Mrs Fullaway's.

"If I had been thinking of getting married I would not have sold it but I have no plans at the moment," says George by means of explanation.

George's club punishment means he misses the pre-season tour that takes in Torquay, Bournemouth, Copenhagen and West Berlin. Then United lose their first League game of the season, at home to Ipswich Town, and results soon make it a season of torment at Old Trafford, unrelieved by the signing of the experienced Welsh bombardier Wyn Davies from Manchester City.

But in September the club's perilous situation is forgotten for one night when Celtic come to Old Trafford for Bobby Charlton's testimonial match. George does not play. He cries off with an injury shortly before kick-off time and goes to The Grapes.

Bill Shankly, whose strong, resilient Liverpool team are destined to win the Football League Championship and UEFA Cup, is at the testimonial. He tells me: "I was standing outside the players' lounge before the game and one of the women who serve the tea asked me if I'd like to go in for a cup. I did, and there was George, sitting on his own. He looked as if he wanted someone to talk to. He looked lonely. I remember how he used to look a few years ago. I remember one time in particular seeing him walk into a place. He was terribly lean and amazingly fit looking. The fitness was shining out of his eyes.

"Anyway, I chatted to him awhile in the players' lounge and then David Sadler came in and they started making a few wisecracks. I didn't know George was going to leave the ground or else I would have told him: 'Look. Don't be silly. I don't care what differences you might have or not have. Get out there and make an appearance. Don't let yourself down.'"

George now has a business address in Manchester, a ground floor office in elegant St John Street, off Deansgate, an area populated by specialists. "I'm the only non-professional here," says George. Cliff Lloyd, the players' counsel, tells me: "George need never fear for the want of help or advice. My office is not far away and my door is always open. If I cannot help him myself, I will make sure he gets the best possible assistance." But George goes his own way.

With United's form ebbing week by week, O'Farrell gambles and United pay £220,000 for the prolific Bournemouth striker Ted MacDougall, whose 103 goals in 146 appearances for the Third Division club fail to prepare him for working under a cloud at Old Trafford.

At the end of October George makes his feelings clear when he says he will not play for United if they are relegated to the Second Division at the end of the season. There is unrest in the United dressing room and the team's condition is becoming critical. George is fined for missing training for a day and a half, and at the end of November the police question him about an incident at Rubens night club involving a 20-year-old girl called Stefanja Sloniecki, from Salford.

George stays away from United and goes to London on December 4. This is the eve of a meeting with the United directors arranged by O'Farrell. George wants to talk with the directors alone to put his side of the story, but during the weekend it is hinted to him that even though he had sympathisers he was unlikely to win if it came to a showdown. George is suspended and put on the transfer list.

George stays in London. On December 6 he is spotted at the exclusive White Elephant in the heart of the capital's clubland where he has a "two hour champagne lunch" with actress Fiona Lewis and actor Ian Lephernis.

They leave in a battered Citroen driven by Miss Lewis with George insisting "I cannot talk about anything" though Mr Lephernis reveals they are shortly to leave for Marbella. George is then driven to a luxury home in Roehampton before finding himself in a flat overlooking the Thames at Cheyne Walk, Chelsea later that evening.

A week later there appears hope of a reconciliation between George and United. It emerges that a meeting has taken place at the home of Sir Matt Busby. George is seen driving to Busby's house in Chorlton-cum-Hardy in a white Rolls Royce. Afterwards, it is revealed that Best "will begin training as soon as possible". Worryingly, United boss O'Farrell says "he knows nothing" about the meeting. It is all too much for Frank McGhee of the Mirror who pens his own George Best fairy tale:

Once upon a time ...

... a First Division footballer stripped and then ridiculed what should have been the love of his life — a game called football.

Then this busy, busy little boy went off to complete in his newspaper column the job of convincing young kids who idolise him that his is an example to follow.

In his newspaper column he revealed that he was fond of booze and birds. He revealed that he despised the club, didn't care for his teammates, and wasn't worried if he never saw another football, scored another goal, or won another medal.

He managed, somehow, to create an impression that he wanted to get away.

But when London clubs — all run by unimaginative fools — did not immediately form a queue to pay a fortune for him – and to him – he said he was sorry

How noble, how self-sacrificing, how decent. His club then, of course, forgave him

They welcomed him back. Start training again, they said. If you don't like the set-up, we can always change it, they said.

We're not proud, they said. Never mind all the things you have written they said. The public will soon forget, they said.

If you don't happen to believe this fairy story, I'm sorry — but at least it might amuse you. It couldn't happen in real life that a player could behave in an outrageous fashion and still be welcomed back by his club. It just is not possible.

But, indeed, fairy tales do not come true. United are deep in relegation trouble when they lose 5-0 at Crystal Palace and the major storm breaks on December 19 at a six-man board meeting at Old Trafford.

George sends a letter saying he is finished with football. The board decide unanimously to fire O'Farrell and tell George that he will never play for United again. They say a decision to leave George on the transfer list and to accept that he will never play another match for the club was taken at a meeting in the morning.

Wilf McGuinness has a place in the sun. He is at this time the manager of Aris Salonika, Greece. He tells me: "Right at this moment I feel very sorry for Frank O'Farrell. I feel sorry for those concerned because it is a bad time for Manchester United. I like to think that the board, having appointed the manager, would stick by him. This would possibly have helped the club. If they went down, well, they went down together. And got up together. That's what I used to think and what I was brought up to believe as a player at United.

"Sometimes I think some people put a lot of faith in players who might not be able to do it anymore. I don't know enough about the internal relationships at the club now, but I wouldn't put the present problems all down to the George Best issue. Of course he's not been right, but he is no more to blame for what has happened than anyone else."

There is a view that Busby ought to have curbed George's way-ward behaviour while still in charge of the team, long before the side peaked as a unit – probably in 1967, the year leading up to European glory – and George was virtually left to carry a side in need of rebuilding.

Busby, in common with most football managers, has dealt with problem players in the past, but none like George, whose celebrity during a time of transformation in youth culture elevated him beyond football norms.

It is also suggested that Sir Matt's continued presence at Old Trafford inhibits his successors, that the task becomes more diffi-cult because the great man casts a shadow. Sir Matt insists that his office door is always open for advice while emphasising that he does not interfere in the running of the team.

Johan Cruyff is the captain of Ajax, of Amsterdam, the World Club Champions. George won a European Cup winners' medal with United in 1968. Johan, a year younger than George, will shortly win his third in a row. Like George, Johan attacks oppos-ing defences with skill and grace, and is richly rewarded for his artistry. Unlike George, Johan is married. His beautiful blonde wife, Danny, is the daughter of a businessman, Cor Coster, who was a dealer in watches and jewellery but now looks after his son-in-law's business interests. The Cruyffs have two daughters, Chantal and Susila, blonde like their mother, and their future is assured by their father's football ability and the channelling of endorsements and other outside interests through Johan Cruyff Publicity, Inc., Amsterdam.

Johan has a classical footballer's background. His father, who died when Johan was 12, was a baker and Johan's mother worked as a cleaner at the Ajax stadium. Johan used to play in a street of the east-side district of Amsterdam. He joined Ajax as a six-year-old cub, did not finish high school, but now lives in luxury in the delightful village of Vinkeveen, 15 miles from Amsterdam.

I ask Johan about George's situation and he tells me: "He is looking for something. Something that isn't there. I know life must be difficult for him, but he must sort himself out before it is too late. I can understand what is happening to Best because a few years ago I was in a similar situation. I just did not know which way my career, or even my life, would go next. I nearly left Ajax and I also had personal problems. But I was lucky because I was able to get good advice from several good friends, people I had known for a long time, people I could trust. When I leave a match or finish training I go home to my wife and family and I leave football behind. Football is never mentioned in my home. I shut the door on my work as soon as I enter my house.

"This means that I have another world outside of football. Somewhere I can go and just be me. I no longer leave the football ground and drift, looking for that something that isn't there."

***

January 11, 1973: Manchester Stipendiary
Magistrate Mr. John Bamber says George,
represented by George Carmen QC, is guilty of
assaulting Stefanja Sloniecka in Rubens night
club the previous November.

Says Mr. Bamber: "I would put the injury at £75. But as she brought about two-thirds of it on her own shoulders, I will make an order for £25.

"She was pretty drunk, in ordinary common parlance. She tried to force her company on Best, who is a celebrity. She is 20, it was 2am, and she was pretty drunk.

"It is clear Best's reaction at first was to ignore her, and that led to her engaging in some crude verbal abuse." (The court hears she called him "an Irish navvy" and a "big-headed bastard".) Then she slapped George's face.

"That is irritating and it was meant to be. But to Best's credit he turned aside and did nothing. This did not satisfy her and she showed signs of doing it again. I am forced to the conclusion that Best responded to this aggravation and provocation by getting hold of her hand, in a manner of self-defence, and with his other free hand struck out at her.

"I accept what a witness said that the matter was not serious and that the injuries had been asked for. Nevertheless the law does not allow one to retaliate in this manner."

XIV

George Best, travel agent

*'We build superstars and then
we knock them down'*

George, The Footballer and The Name, has turned his back on
potential earnings of £1 million over the next five years. His way-
ward ways have cost him a conservative estimate of at least
£100,000 in lost earnings over the past three years. That is to say
money lost through broken appointments and contracts not
renewed. A recent example of this was when representatives of a
leading film company paid a fruitless visit to the office in St. John
Street.

They wanted to make a film of George's life story and were prepared to pay George about £60,000 to give them the go ahead, cast-
ing an actor to play his role. George was in town, but did not see
them.

In another story that appears away from the sports pages in the
newspaper, a waxwork model of George in a Blackpool exhibition
is replaced with football's rising young superstar, Kevin Keegan of
Liverpool. It is a sign that the times are changing.

Around this time I upset my sports editor, David Nicholls, by
refusing to disclose the source of a story, firmly committed to pro-
tecting a contact. Arnold Howe, the Express's North East sports
correspondent, has retired and is in Manchester for a farewell
party. I arrive at the pub and David is standing at the bar with

Arnold. I join them, and David raises the subject of the source of my story again.

"I don't know," he says, "I must be doing something wrong if one of my own staff doesn't trust me." While David is talking my eyes are focussed on a silver tankard on the bar in front of him, a gift from Arnold inscribed, "To a great boss".

Arnold is right, David is a great boss. In fact he offered me the opportunity of succeeding Arnold in the North East, which I declined because I wanted to remain closer to the success of the football clubs and the hub of the newspaper industry in Manchester. George's agent, Ken Stanley, was among those who advised me against the move.

Arnold Howe, a slight, dapper former Daily Herald sports writer in Manchester, recalled returning to the city to cover a match between United and Sunderland at Old Trafford. "After the match I was a bit late getting down to the dressing room area for the interviews," he said. "I had to stand at the back of the throng of reporters listening to Matt Busby. After a while Matt paused, looked across, and said, 'Hello, Arnold'. I couldn't believe it. He hadn't seen me for years. He made me feel ten foot tall."

Football times are changing in Manchester. Tommy Docherty, a tough, dedicated Scot with a short fuse, takes over United, accepting the job with a handshake in chairman Louis Edwards' car as he is driven from Manchester's Ringway airport. Docherty puts the team on a course of iron and keeps them in the First Division. Joe Mercer, a soccer statesman, has left Manchester City and is lending warmth, humour and experience to Coventry City. Malcolm Allison, "Big Mal" of the Cockney swagger and progressive, vibrant, flexible football mind, is also leaving Manchester City, bound for Crystal Palace and the Second Division.

George has changed the blue Jaguar for a leased white Rolls Royce. He has toured America and is now piecing together new ventures. The boutique no longer carries his name, but next door to it in Motor Street is a travel business. Frank Evans, a young man with an adventurous spirit that led him to the bullrings of Spain, and Malcolm Wagner are partners with George. Frank was manager of the boutique when Malcolm Mooney left. George hopes to open a night club and write a book.

The nightclub is to be named Slack Alice's, after a character created by the camp comedian Larry Grayson, though one of George's friends tells me, "We thought of calling it something like Parasites, but that would only be knocking ourselves."

It is not long before there are stories that George is making another comeback. Allison's Palace would like him and there are reports of interest from Swansea to Chelsea. Tommy Docherty says that although George will never play for United again he would like to see the boy back in football. But before any negotiations can be started George must first report to the club for training. "I miss success," George tells me. My feelings are clear. I write:

Malcolm Allison, Tommy Docherty, I and millions would love to see soccer enriched again by the talent of George Best. I regret we never shall, because I doubt that the talent still exists as we knew it. George will not settle for less than the greatness he bestowed upon Manchester United and the world for eight seasons. He will never push himself hard enough to become little more than an average First Division player. And that, I fear, is the best he can now hope to be.

Pride, plus a natural sense of loss of his place as an idol at the pinnacle of our national game, make George think about making a comeback. It is only a thought. George will soon be 27 years old; a babe in terms of a lifetime, but middle-aged in terms of football. He could go to

*South Africa or the United States and still look an
outstanding player and be a big attraction. But the hard
and fast world of top-class professional football in this
country would perhaps be too much for him to reproduce
the form that made him a superstar. At the back of his
mind he must know that it is better to leave soccer lovers
with a glorious memory of his true ability than tarnish
that memory with an abortive attempt at a comeback. He
would never forgive himself for that. George misses
success. I hope he has enough sense to avoid failure.*

I am seated in the back of Frank O'Farrell's maroon Jaguar XJ6,
having accepted a lift to a match at Everton. Frank is still between
jobs and is keeping in touch with the game.

"How's George?" he asks.

"Fine, I think," I reply. "You know how it is."

"Yes," he says. "It's such a pity. You know, I was criticised for
buying forwards instead of more defenders, but I felt George needed help up front, someone to take the weight off him and to take
over a bit of the responsibility on the days when things weren't
coming off for him. People have said one player doesn't make a
team, but there were times when he did win matches for us because
of his great ability to break stalemate situations.

"That game against Sheffield United was a good example. It
would have helped if the atmosphere in the dressing room had been
better. And you only seemed to hear that George's private life was
getting out of hand when things were not coming off for him on the
field. It was rarely mentioned when things were going well."

Mario Zagalo is the team manager of Brazil, the World Cup
holders. He controls players of rubber-limbed brilliance and explo-
sive temperament and is planning the defence of the championship
in the 1974 finals in West Germany without his genius, Pele,

scorer of more than 1,000 goals but now retired from international football.

Zagalo, grey, small and sprightly, echoes O'Farrell when I ask, through an interpreter, for an opinion about George. "I can talk about Best the footballer and say: 'Yes, a great player', but I cannot talk about Best's private life because that is not my business. So judge him as a player and not as a person. That is his business. We all live our own lives," he says.

The events of the first part of 1973 prompt sports reporters to talk of the "Year of the Underdog": George Foreman has played basketball with Joe Frazier to win the world heavyweight title, Ken Norton has outpointed Muhammad Ali and broken the poet's jaw, and Sunderland have beaten Leeds United to win the FA Cup.

It is not a vintage year for George. He takes a set of weights to his digs in an attempt to will the sleek, hard line back to his body and reports to United for training. For a day.

In spring Bobby Charlton retires as a player to become manager of Preston North End.

There is a story that with Bobby gone George wants to play for United again, but he continues to be George Best, travel agent.

A client is keen to see holiday accommodation in Spain and wants his family to go with him. It is a large family and, for reasons of safety, the client takes the precaution of arranging separate flights. He goes from Birmingham with the older children and his wife from London with their baby. George and Malcolm Wagner are with her at Heathrow. There is a long delay and George becomes impatient and threatens to leave at half-hourly intervals. People stare at this unusual domestic scene.

But George is still there when the flight is called.

While on another business trip to Spain he is rushed back to Manchester for treatment to what is reported to be thrombosis of a calf.

A bed is available at Ancoats Hospital and he spends a couple of weeks there, leaving in time for his 27th birthday.

"I knew it would catch up with you in the end," I joke with him. "You can't live like that and get away with it. I'll never end up like that. Colds and catarrh, that's me."

George laughs and says: "Boring things like that."

I consider the extremes of glowing praise and biting criticism and reflect on something Frank O'Farrell said at the height of the crisis: "It is a great tragedy. Inside the club he is perfect. He trains well. He is likeable. All the trouble happens outside. Who is to blame? I suppose everybody. We build superstars and then knock them down. Perhaps it's society. I don't know."

George helped, but we certainly knocked him down.

Postscript

It is early evening on June 19, 1973, and I go to the travel agency in Motor Street, The Village, Manchester. Parked outside is the blue E-Type Jaguar with a V12 engine (George's white Rolls became too clear a target for vandals). With George are Malcolm Wagner and Frank Evans. George has had a copy of this book for exactly a week and has just returned from London and a visit to Mike Parkinson, who is helping to put together George's autobiography. When Malcolm and Frank leave I ask George for his reaction to what I have written, emphasising that I have tried to report the events as I saw them as accurately as possible.

"I don't want to say anything about it because I am writing a book of my own," he says. I press him and he adds: "I am immune from anything that is written about me unless I have written it myself, and have been for many years. Too much has been said and written about me by too many people. It goes in one ear and out the other, or I read it and it doesn't register. It has no effect. It does not even interest me."

Would it interest him if it was about another player?

"Not really. I've been too close to the game and its incidents."

I ask if he has any objection to the book or anything in particular I have written and he says: "I have no objection to any book written about me. You could have called me a so-and-so on the first page and I wouldn't have objected."

I ask if he thinks the book is honest and he replies: "Oh, yes, it's honest. If it was dishonest you wouldn't have got through that door. But I won't go into any detail about it unless I do it in my own book. That is the only book that has any meaning for me because I know I will be able to believe every word that's in it!"

We discuss his relationship with journalists in recent years and I ask what troubled him most about newspapers. "A lot of things," he says. I ask about his future.

No more football?

"No more football."

What then?

"I have a few plans and I just hope they work out over the next few year," he says.

And your book?

"It's going to be a bomb! Mike Parkinson has been like a psychiatrist."

He says he appreciates the fact that I have allowed him to see my book, and before I leave I ask him if he has any regrets about the way things have turned out for him.

He shakes his head and says: "No. None at all. You see, I've always made up my own mind about things. I've always made my own decisions. Some might be right and some might be wrong. When you make your own decisions you have only yourself to blame."

August 27, 1973

The inevitable happens. Manchester United chairman Louis Edwards says the club would like George to start training again and the question of his playing for United would be left to the board of directors.

The following day George, on holiday in Majorca, says he would like to give it another try.

It has been a summer of high finance for superstars. Gunter Netzer, the leggy, blond midfielder from West Germany, has collected £150,000 from a move to Real Madrid. Johan Cruyff is waiting to leave Amsterdam to join Barcelona in a deal worth £461,000 to Ajax and almost as much to the player.

These figures have not escaped the notice of United, or George. There is the stir of a new season, and the stir of a new season will always rekindle memories of George Best. *15

Che Sera.

Notes

*1 **(page 15)**

George's brother, Ian Busby Best, had not been born.

*2 **(page 15)**

This brought me into contact with two football managers whose only similarity was that both were successful. Bill Shankly, at Liverpool, lived and breathed football, famously saying – and only half joking – that the game is more important than life and death. Harry Catterick, at Everton, was withdrawn by comparison, particularly in his relationship with the Press.

Shankly virtually marched me out of Anfield during one of our early encounters – the day after Roger Hunt tossed his shirt into the dugout after becoming the first Liverpool player to be substituted – but when Bill retired I was honoured to collaborate with him in the writing of his autobiography.

Catterick – "I'm a miserable looking beggar to begin with" – held the view that a football club and its supporters is a family: "And like most families, it's OK to have a go at each other but not for outsiders to have a go at us."

I was pleasantly surprised to receive a letter from Harry after he left the manager's office at Everton expressing "appreciation for the friendly association we had in the course of business."

*3 **(page 15)**

On the subject of embarrassing moments, after covering a match between Newcastle United and Ipswich Town on a frosty afternoon in 1969 I found myself sharing a rail carriage with Don Revie, Syd Owen and David Herd on the journey home. Leeds United's match at Old Trafford had been called off because of an icy pitch and Revie, the manager, and Owen, the coach, had decided to go to Newcastle to scout future opponents. Herd, the former United striker, was then with Stoke City.

I was seated next to Owen, facing Revie and Herd. As a boy I remembered David playing alongside his father Alec for Stockport County, my home town team. In those days I was lucky enough to watch Manchester United's "Busby Babes" and the Manchester City team in which Revie played the deep-laying centre forward role styled after the Hungarian Nandor Hidegkuti.

We discussed the Hungarian team that defeated England 6-3 at Wembley in 1953, and I said, "And the next year, remember, they beat us 7-1 in Budapest."

"I remember all right," said Syd, "I was the bloody centre half."

*4 **(page 19)**

There was an amusing sequel to this more than twenty years later when I was in Madrid to cover the 1982 World Cup final as a Daily Mail sports feature writer. As reporters sunbathed at a hotel swimming pool, one man looked familiar. It was Tommy Anderson, who was working for the Australian office of an international sports news agency. Jeff Powell, the Mail's football correspondent, persuaded the reluctant Tommy to relate the aftermath of a riot on the terraces when England played Argentina in a world youth tournament in Sydney.

Having returned home after filing his report on the match and the riot, Tommy received a fax from the agency's Buenos Aires office, asking: "Was Malvenos responsible for riot at match?" To which Tommy replied: "According to my notes, Malvenos did not play."

* 5 **(page 34)**
In the 1954 film The Barefoot Contessa, "Che Sera, Sera" was the family motto of the character played by Rossano Brazzi. Doris Day sang the song "Che Sera, Sera" in the 1956 Alfred Hitchcock film *The Man Who Knew Too Much.* The music was by Bernard Herrmann and the lyrics by Ray Evans and Jay Livingston, who changed the Italian "Che" to the Spanish "Que" because more people spoke Spanish in the United States.

*6 **(page 36)**
In 2010 Starbucks stands where Edwardia and the Village Barber used to be.

*7 **(page 37)**
While Germaine Greer did not burn her bra in front of George in the Brown Bull, the icon of Women's Lib wrote in The Independent in 2005 about being tapped on the arm by George while she was standing at the bar in 1968. The pub is a few minutes away from Granada TV, where Greer was employed two days a week making a television series with Kenny Everett.

"I turned round to find George Best smiling at me. The fact that his eyes were on a level with my chin lessoned their impact, but not much... George was speaking. Even when my ears weren't drumming I had to struggle to understand his Belfast-speak, delivered as usual very fast from behind his teeth. What he was saying was, I worked out, 'Why d'ye not fancy me?'

"Not fancy you? Don't be ridiculous, George. Everybody fancies you.'"

"So why not you?'"

"'I do fancy you, George.'"

"'So why d'ye do nothing about it?'"

"Because I'm not a fool, George. Every time you come in here you've got a different blonde on your arm."

"I decided to tease George, if only because he was teasing me. said: 'Besides, there's someone in the team I fancy more.'

"It worked. George was genuinely astounded. 'Who is it? Who is it?'"

"Guess."

"George went right through the team: Alex Stepney? Tony Dunne? Billy Foulkes? Shay Brennan? Paddy Crerand? Bobby Charlton? Brian Kidd? John Aston? No to all of them. George was stumped.

"'I'm not surprised you can't work it out,' I said reprovingly. 'He's been playing opposite you and you haven't seen him yet, let alone passed him the ball.' This was always my beef with George as a player. If he got the ball he kept it."

"George eventually figured out who had taken my fancy and, typically, went out of his way to make sure we got a chance to get together, but that's a different story. I never did get to tell George how it turned out, and if I didn't tell him, there's not much point in telling anyone else."

*8 (page 41)
Malcolm Mooney was killed in a road accident at Mere Corner, Cheshire.

*9 (page 43)
In August 1979, after Denis had retired and was commentating for

BBC radio, I interviewed him for The Guardian when his autobiography was due to be published. He expanded on his desire as a player for privacy away from football. "As soon as a match was over my aim was to have a bath, get dressed, and go home as soon as possible. I didn't want to hang about. Off the field I was a different person altogether. But I think all of us change our personalities to fit different situations.

"I never liked watching myself play on television. I found it embarrassing. The character who was supposed to be me on the screen wasn't really me at all. He couldn't be, throwing a punch at someone, glaring at the linesman, arguing with the referee and making rude signs. I didn't behave like that in real life. I could understand people watching me and saying, 'What's he up to? Who does he think he is?' because I used to think the same things myself. 'Oh to see ourselves as others see us,' as Rabbi Burns said.

On Best, he said: "I understand a lot of what happened to George. When I was young I went through a lot of the same things. Like George, I used to find it difficult to say no to people when I really meant no. I would find it easier to to say yes even if I knew I probably wouldn't turn up for an appointment later."

* 10 (page 70)

Malcolm's successful partnership with Joe Mercer at City ends in acrimony. With Joe in the manager's office, Malcolm's innovative coaching skills produced a team that, between 1965 and 1970, raised City from the Second Division and won the First Division Championship, the FA Cup, the League Cup and the European Cup Winners' Cup.

During this time, Joe was occasionally called upon to intercede when his outspoken partner's barbed comments upset rival managers, Everton's Harry Catterick being among those offended.

Malcolm's ambition to become City's manager and to be given

the credit he believes is his due for the club's years of glory, leads him to side with a successful takeover group, and Joe moves on to become the manager at Coventry City.

"Malcolm and I were like Flanagan and Allen," Joe tells me, "but I was never sure which of us was Flanagan."

Harry Godwin, City's chief scout, the man who helped to supply the players vital to the club's success – David Wagstaffe, Mike Summerbee, Colin Bell, Francis Lee, Mike Doyle, Willie Donachie, plus a fine supporting cast – was particularly disappointed by the managerial split. "I mean, how can you have Morecambe without Wise?" he tells me later. "Unfortunately it got to the stage where Malcolm had more hangers-on than a Bombay tram." My first encounter with Harry was when he went to Belfast in the late 1960s to assess the Glentoran midfield player Tommy Jackson, later to play for Manchester United. Harry, a United supporter for 30 years, left his job as a clerk at Metrovickers to become a full-time scout at the age of 50, when George Poyser was City's manager.

"I thought I'd joined a fire station," Harry says. "A couple of days after I decided to go full-time scouting, City sacked their coach, Jimmy Meadows. A few days after that, George was sacked, and I wondered if I'd done the right thing. Joe Mercer brought the place alive again."

Shortly afterwards Malcolm Allison arrived as Joe's assistant. "I opened the door to Mal in the general office," Harry recalls, "and he said, 'I want to see the secretary.' I looked at him and said, 'You're that bloody nutcase from Plymouth who was at Bury the other week,' and Mal said, 'Thanks very much.' I said, 'Well, if you'd told me two weeks ago that you'd been working here, I'd have stayed at Metros'."

One night the Express receives a telephone tip-off that a Manchester City player has been involved in a road accident and I phone Harry to see if he knows anything about it. "Not a thing, John," Harry says. "I just hope it's a hoax. I'll tell you one thing, though. If this conversation goes on much longer I'll probably be in the News of the World – I'm standing here without any clothes on." Happily, the tip-off turns out to be a hoax.

* 11 **(page 84)**

If Ali is not at home he invariably leaves a number where he can be contacted. As a result I am able to speak with him before and after several of his fights. I hesitate to use the word interview, because as soon as I introduce a topic Ali does all the talking.

The day after Joe Frazier lost the world heavyweight title to George Foreman in Jamaica in 1973 I asked Ali for his thoughts. "Joe Frazier is a fool," he growled down the telephone. "If he was going to get beat he should have let me beat him – that way we would both have made a lot of money. I know I'll beat George Foreman because he fights like a wash-er-wom-an."

Ali paused and said, "Say, what's that newspaper of yours?"

"The Daily Express," I said.

"Well, you sure are getting a good interview."

* 12 **(page 89)**

This comes eighteen days after Stoke City, one of the 12 original Football League clubs, win the first major trophy in their history, defeating Chelsea in the League Cup final, 2-1. Terry Conroy heads Stoke's first goal and creates the winner for George Eastham, and I am reminded of my time working in Belfast when Conroy played for Glentoran and Eastham's father, George Sr, was the manager of Ards.

Conroy played for Glentoran in a 1-1 draw against Glasgow Rangers in 1966, in the first leg of a first round European Cup-Winners Cup tie, after which I was rebuffed, shall we say, by the

Rangers manager, Scot Symon, when I sought his thoughts about Conroy's talent. There was much gloom in the Rangers camp when a group of Irish sport writers visited their hotel (having first celebrated with Glentoran) to drink and commiserate with some of the Rangers officials. One of these, who was wearing a grey houndstooth suit which had seen better days, lingered longer than the rest, until the puckish Jack Milligan, of the Daily Mirror, leaned over and said, "What you need is a new team – and a new suit."

George Eastham Sr, a former England international who played for Bolton and Blackpool, persuaded Tom Finney to step out of retirement in 1963 to play his only European Cup tie – for Distillery in a 3-3 draw with Benfica. As the player-manager of Ards, George Sr played alongside George Jr, and he was later proud of his son's stand against Newcastle United in 1960, leading to the end of the League's retain-and-transfer system by which players were bound to clubs.

* 13 **(page 123)**
Kevin Keegan, on a later visit to my home, autographed the back of the frame, "to Christopher, from Uncle Kevin Keegan".

* 14 **(page 125)**
Peter Jackson was an excellent photographer and a splendid colleague. A few years after our trip to Majorca he died tragically while on holiday after falling from a hotel window and being trapped in a narrow space between two walls. Tony Knowles, the snooker player from Bolton, was among the first on the scene, making a forlorn rescue attempt.

* 15 **(page 151)**
The prodigal's return to Old Trafford provided a few nostalgic glimpses of his former genius before self-destruction prevailed

again. George's last match for United was in a 3-0 defeat at Queen's Park Rangers on New Year's Day, 1974.

From that point George became a football nomad for the rest of his career, meandering off to share what remained of his talent with a variety of clubs, such as Dunstable, Stockport and Cork Celtic, a memorable renaissance at Fulham in the company of Rodney Marsh and Bobby Moore, and on to Los Angeles Aztecs, Fort Lauderdale, Hibernian, San Jose Earthquakes, Bournemouth and Brisbane.

"I will always remember George's brilliance," Bill Shankly told me when I collaborated with the Liverpool legend on his memoirs. "He knew what other players were capable of, and, when he was at his best, he was waiting for people to make mistakes. He knew who was liable to make them. One day at Old Trafford we took a throw-in that I had banned – a throw straight across the face of the pitch at the halfway line – and though I shouted, our fellow did the same thing again. George was reading it, and he flustered us into making a mistake, sprinted through, picked up the ball and scored a goal. He made it happen. He started the trouble and then finished it off. When George played his last game for Manchester United at Anfield he didn't play well and the crowd laughed at him. That was a terrible thing – because nobody could laugh at George Best."

George just wanted to be remembered as a great footballer, a wish that was respected when he was given what amounted to a state funeral in Belfast. An outpouring of grief was mingled with fond recollections of his finest moments on the field of play.

It has often been said that it was a shame he squandered his talent, a rebuke that fails to take into account the fact that George made a total of 470 appearances for United between 1963 and the dawning of 1974 and scored 179 goals. Fortunately archives of film exist as reminders of his magic under pressure with a ball at his feet.

Mirror Sport

Saturday, May 20, 1972
Telephone : (STD code 01)—353 0246

BOUVERIE

12-1 NAP!
57-1 DOUBLE!!
33-1 WINNER!!!

RACING MIRROR: PAGES 26-29

BE OUR GUEST
AT THE MUNICH
OLYMPICS.
Free trips for
eleven couples
Details next week

PETER WILSON

REPORTS FROM AMERICA
ON THE WORLD
HEAVYWEIGHT FIGHT

IN MIRROR SPORT NEXT WEEK

HAS BEST WALKED OUT OF SOCCER?

Two quit England's game after ban threat

From CHRIS LANDER

Capetown, Friday

TWO coloured Rugby players have decided not to play against the English Rugby tourists here on Monday.

The Moerat brothers, Ighraam and Marwaan, withdrew from the South African Rugby Federation team after they were told by their club, Paarl, today: "If you play we will ban you for two years."

Ighraam, 18-year-old flanker, and Marwaan, 24-year-old lock, both came to Britain with the Proteas in December.

Both are the coloured anti-apartheid group in the Cape Province.

Supporters of the Labour Party Council, the opposition to the Coloureds' Representative Council, are planning demonstrations at the Athlone Stadium on Monday.

Jobs

They want multi-racial teams and claim that England's programme here merely supports the present laws of apartheid in sport.

There have been open threats to players and their families, and some players have been told: "Your jobs are in danger if you play against England."

The Proteas have been victim-...

GEORGE BEST ... pictured on a sunshine holiday in Spain last year.

STRAIN ON THE STARS

By ALAN BALL

JUST three more matches to go, three home internationals to relieve some of...

are the two most obvious heartaches...

By HARRY MILLER

GEORGE BEST was on the Costa del Sol in Spain last night, clearly determined to play no part in today's home international Soccer championship.

While his Irish team-mates were at Troon, preparing for this afternoon's game against Scotland, a sun-tanned Best sat in the lounge of a five-star hotel in Marbella.

He refused to comment on growing speculation that he is prepared to quit the game that has built him into a super-star.

Back at Troon, Ireland were ready to wait until the last possible moment before calling him out of this afternoon's match.

But it now seems certain that many play without him.

Relaxed

For Best, accompanied by two...

'In Spain to relax' he says

—and lend massive weight to the theory that he is finished with football.

Earlier in the day Derek and were bending over backwards to avoid asking Irwin who should have joined them at mid-day on Thursday.

Needed

Skipper Derek Dougan "There is no feeling among the players that George has let them

"It is a great player there is on before in football than in fall song. We said later: "The asked me to leave go open. I HAVE

McGarry to stay!

BILL McGARRY is staying with Wolves. And that means Coventry City must start their search for a manager all over again.

A four-hour board meeting at Molineux yesterday ended with the announcement that McGarry had accepted a new contract.

McGarry told us later: "I'm now looking forward to all the Wolves building we have achieved over four years."

Coventry could now switch their attention to a young boss—such as Orient's George Petchey.

HARRY MILLER

WILL IT WORK

THE WAYWARD BEST...

HE SAID:

GEORGE BEST, Manchester United's repentant runaway, has been given his last chance by the club.

From O'Farrell, the manager who has had to try to pin him without risking favour of his patron, made that clear last night.

O'Farrell's promise for United's match is clearly a matter of waiting to see whether George...

By JOHN BEAN

BEST IS ORDERED OFF!

United ace goes after flare-up with referee

How Kirby can afford to smile 5p on.

'They've been

THREAT TO STRIP FRAZIER OF TITLE

Back to jail for loser

From GORDON GREGOR, New York, Friday

Evonne set for another big pay-ou

HAMMERS DOWN AGAIN—AND TAYLOR RUNS INTO TROUBLE

FIVE BOOKED AS SPURS STRUGGLE

Pathetic Palace on a four-goal loser

COLCHESTER CUP HEROES STORM ON

George Best
timeline
1971-1973

(All matches English First Division unless stated)

July 31, 1971: *Halifax Town 2, Man Utd 1 (Watney Cup).*
Best scores United's goal
Aug 14, 1971: *Derby 2, Man Utd 2*
Aug 18, 1971: *Chelsea 2, Man Utd 3*
Aug 20, 1971: *Man Utd 3, Arsenal 1*
Aug 23,1971: *Man Utd 3, West Brom 1. Best scores two*
Aug 28, 1971: *Wolves 1, Man Utd 1. Best scores*
Aug 31, 1971: *Everton 1, Man Utd 0*
Sept 4, 1971: *Man Utd 1, Ipswich 0. Best scores direct*
from a corner kick, which Ipswich manager Bobby Robson
dismisses as a freak goal
Sept 7, 1971: *Ipswich 1, Man Utd 3 (League Cup, Best 2)*
Sept 11, 1971: *Crystal Palace 1, Man Utd 3*
Sept 13, 1971: *Best attends FA disciplinary hearing following*
his red card at Chelsea. He escapes without further suspension
Sept 18, 1971: *Man Utd 4, West Ham 2. Best scores hat-trick*
Sept 22, 1971: *Northern Ireland lose 1-0 to Russia in the*
Lenin Stadium
Sept 25, 1971: *Liverpool 2, Man Utd 2. The Daily Express begins*

to run a George Best soccer skills strip in the newspaper

Oct 1, 1971: *Best reveals in his column that he has been offered a bit part in a film alongside Alf Garnett by his friend, the writer Johnny Speight*

Oct 2, 1971: *Man Utd 2, Sheff Utd 0. Best's virtuoso performance helps United close the gap on the visitors, who are the surprise leaders of the First Division. Best clashes with the Blades' Trevor Hockey but escapes punishment, later playing down the incident in his column*

Oct 6, 1971: *Man Utd 1, Burnley 1 (League Cup)*

Oct 8, 1971: *Best is among the players lined up to appear in the Daily Express indoor five-a-side tournament at Wembley*

Oct 9, 1971: *Huddersfield 0, Man Utd 3. Best scores again*

Oct 13, 1971: *United deny Best permission to play for Northern Ireland against Russia in Belfast after he receives death threats. Northern Ireland draw 1-1 and go out of the European Nations Cup*

Oct 16, 1971: *Man Utd 1, Derby 0. Best scores the winner*

Oct 18, 1971: *Burnley 0, Man Utd 1 (League Cup)*

Oct 22, 1971: *Best warns about the dangers of drug taking in an outspoken Daily Express column*

Oct 23, 1971: *Newcastle 0, Man Utd 1. Best scores the only goal of the game despite receiving a threat that he will be shot during the match*

Oct 27, 1971: *Man Utd 0, Stoke 0 (League Cup)*

Oct 30, 1971: *Man Utd 0, Leeds 1*

Nov 6, 1971: *Man City 3, Man Utd 3*

Nov 8, 1971: *Stoke 0, Man Utd 0 (League Cup)*

Nov 13, 1971: *Man Utd 3, Tottenham 1*

Nov 15, 1971: *Stoke City 2, Man Utd 1 (League Cup). United lose in third League Cup tie with Stoke but Best on scoresheet*

Nov 17, 1971: *Best appears on 'This Is Your Life'*

Nov 20, 1971: *Man Utd 3, Leicester 2*
Nov 26, 1971: *Best reveals in his column that he has been offered £10,000 to play six games in South Africa after the season ends. He also complains about ex-girlfriends who have recently gone public to talk about their affairs with him, notably Susan George and Jackie Glass*
Nov 27, 1971: *Southampton 2, Man Utd 5. Best scores his second hat-trick of the season*
Dec 4, 1971: *Man Utd 3, Nottingham Forest 2*
Dec 10, 1971: *Best meets Jackie Stewart, who receives the Daily Express Sportsman of the Year trophy*
Dec 11, 1971: *Stoke 1, Man Utd 1*
Dec 15, 1971: *Best comes second to Princess Anne in BBC Sports Personality of the Year*
Dec 18, 1971: *Ipswich 0, Man Utd 0*
Dec 24, 1971: *Best dismisses claims in his column that he could be the first £500,000 footballer*
Dec 27, 1971: *Man Utd 2, Coventry 2*
Dec 31, 1971: *Best reveals that a fan has sent United boss Frank O'Farrell a letter saying he saw him come out of a nightclub at 5am the night before a match. Best says this is "rubbish"*
Jan 1, 1972: *West Ham 3, Man Utd 0*
Jan 4, 1972: *Best misses a week of training*
Jan 7, 1972: *There is a suggestion that Great Britain will put up a football team to be managed by Sir Matt Busby to contest a 'mini-World Cup' in Brazil. The Daily Express asks readers to name their GB Lions team. Best is the only player who is named on every single entry*
Jan 8, 1972: *Man Utd 1, Wolves 3. Best is dropped for the game after missing training. He spends a weekend in London with Miss Great Britain Carolyn Moore and there is speculation that they are planning to get married, which they both deny*

Jan 10, 1972: Best reports back to Old Trafford where he is given extra training as punishment. He is also fined two weeks' wages and ordered to leave Che Sera and move back in with his old landlady, Mrs Fullaway, although it soons becomes apparent that he is not giving up his new house. Best is asked to go on David Frost's television show but he refuses

Jan 15, 1972: Southampton 1, Man Utd 1 (FA Cup)

Jan 19, 1972: Man Utd 4, Southampton 1 (FA Cup). Best scores two goals but makes an 'obscene gesture' towards the press which puts him back in the headlines

Jan 22, 1972: Man Utd 0, Chelsea 1

Jan 28, 1972: Best suggests he may quit the game 'when he reaches 30'

Jan 29, 1972: West Brom 2, Man Utd 1

Feb 5, 1972: Preston 0, Man Utd 2 (FA Cup)

Feb 12, 1972: Man Utd 0, Newcastle 2

Feb 16, 1972: Northern Ireland 1, Spain 1 (Hull). Best tells John Roberts that he is tired of playing in a poor Manchester United side and wants to leave the club

Feb 19, 1972: Leeds 5, Man Utd 1

Feb 26, 1972: Man Utd 0, Middlesbrough 0 (FA Cup)

Feb 29, 1972: Middlesbrough 0, Man Utd 3 (FA Cup)

Mar 4, 1972: Tottenham 2, Man Utd 0

Mar 8, 1972: Man Utd 0, Everton 0

Mar 9, 1972: Transfer deadline day. United have signed Martin Buchan and Ian Storey-Moore

Mar 11, 1972: Man Utd 2, Huddersfield 0

Mar 18, 1972: Man Utd 1, Stoke 1 (FA Cup)

Mar 22, 1972: Stoke 2, Man Utd 1 (FA Cup)

Mar 25, 1972: Man Utd 4, Crystal Palace 0

Apr 1, 1972: Coventry 2, Man Utd 3

Apr 3, 1972: Man Utd 0, Liverpool 3

Apr 4, 1972: *Sheff Utd 1, Man Utd 1*

Apr 8, 1972: *Leicester 2, Man Utd 0*

Apr 12, 1972: *Man Utd 1, Man City 3*

Apr 15, 1972: *Man Utd 3, Southampton 2*

Apr 22, 1972: *Nottingham Forest 0, Man Utd 0*

Apr 25, 1972: *Arsenal 3, Man Utd 0*

Apr 29, 1972: *Man Utd 3, Stoke 0*

May 1, 1972: *Plays in Uwe Seeler's testimonial for a Rest of Europe side against Hamburg SV*

May 20, 1972: *Best does not turn up for Northern Ireland duty in Glasgow and is later tracked down to Marbella. He holds a 26th birthday party where he announces that he is to retire from football. Northern Ireland lose 2-0 to Scotland as the British Home Championships kick off*

May 23, 1972: *Matt Busby denies trying to set up a private meeting with Best to talk things over. There is fierce criticism of Best's actions from Northern Ireland. England 0, Northern Ireland 1*

May 24, 1972: *Best tells the press that United's lack of success is the reason why he is quitting and that had they qualified for Europe he would have stayed for "at least one more year". He also says that he wished he would have played abroad instead of in England, saying that English players have to play too many games*

May 27, 1972: *Wales 0, Northern Ireland 0. Northern Ireland finish their Home Championship campaign in third position behind England and Scotland but in front of Wales*

May 31, 1972: *Ajax retain the European Cup, defeating Inter Milan 2-0. They win the trophy again a year later*

June 2, 1972: *Best flies out to Majorca dismissing speculation that he is planning to return to United*

July 7, 1972: *Best announces he will play for United again. He* *flies home and is ordered into lodgings with Pat Crerand. This does not last long and Best moves back in with Mrs Fullaway. He is suspended for two weeks for breaching his contract*

Aug 12, 1972: *Man Utd 1, Ipswich 2 (Start of 1972-73 season)*

Aug 15, 1972: *Liverpool 2, Man Utd 0*

Aug 19, 1972: *Everton 2, Man Utd 0*

Aug 23, 1972: *Man Utd 1, Leicester 1. Best scores first goal of the season*

Aug 26, 1972: *Man Utd 0, Arsenal 0*

Aug 30, 1972: *Man Utd 0, Chelsea 0*

Sept 2, 1972: *West Ham 2, Man Utd 2. Best and Ian Storey-Moore on target*

Sept 6, 1972: *Oxford 2, Man Utd 2 (League Cup)*

Sept 9, 1972: *Man Utd 0, Coventry 1*

Sept 12, 1972: *Man Utd 3, Oxford 1 (League Cup). Best scores twice*

Sept 16, 1972: *Wolves 2, Man Utd 0*

Sept 23, 1972: *Man Utd 3, Derby 0. New signing Wyn Davies makes his debut*

Sept 28, 1972: *United sign Ted MacDougall for £220,000*

Sept 30, 1972: *Sheff Utd 1, Man Utd 0*

Oct 3, 1972: *Bristol Rovers 1, Man Utd 1 (League Cup)*

Oct 7, 1972: *West Brom 2, Man Utd 2. Best on target*

Oct 11, 1972: *Man Utd 1, Bristol Rovers 2 (League Cup)*

Oct 14, 1972: *Man Utd 1, Birmingham 0*

Oct 17, 1972: *Best is mobbed by Bulgarian fans as he arrives in Sofia. According to press it is "the most boisterous reception a British player has ever received in an Iron Curtain country"*

Oct 18, 1972: *Northern Ireland lose 3-0 to Bulgaria in Sofia. Best is sent off*

Oct 21, 1972: *Newcastle 2, Man Utd 1*

Oct 28, 1972: *Man Utd 1, Tottenham 4. Two days after the game,*

Best announces that he will move from the club if United are relegated

Nov 4, 1972: *Leicester 2, Man Utd 2. Best and Wyn Davies score. It is to be Best's last goal of the season for United*

Nov 11, 1972: *Man Utd 2, Liverpool 0*

Nov 18, 1972: *Man City 3, Man Utd 0*

Nov 22, 1972: *Best fined by United for missing training*

Nov 25, 1972: *Man Utd 2, Southampton 1. This is to be Best's last appearance for United in the 1972-73 season. For the final few games he has switched from number 10 to number seven*

Nov 29, 1972: *Has face to face talks with manager Frank O'Farrell after again missing training. He is dropped from the team. Newspaper reports suggest he could be transfer-listed*

Dec 2, 1972: *Norwich 0, Man Utd 2*

Dec 4, 1972: *Best is seen at a London nightclub after leaving Manchester without permission from the club*

Dec 5, 1972: *Best suspended by United for two weeks and put on the transfer list, a fee of £300,000 on his head*

Dec 6, 1972: *Real Madrid express an interest in signing Best. Barcelona and Valencia, managed by Best's footballing idol, Alfredo Di Stefano, are also said to be in the hunt*

Dec 7, 1972: *Ambitious Third Division Bournemouth, managed by John Bond, are reported to be ready to join the chase for Best, using funds from the sale of Ted MacDougall*

Dec 9, 1972: *Man Utd 0, Stoke 2*

Dec 11, 1972: *Derby County, Manchester City and New York Cosmos also declare an interest in signing Best*

Dec 15, 1972: *Following a meeting with Sir Matt Busby, Best resumes training*

Dec 16, 1972: *Crystal Palace 5, Man Utd 0*

Dec 19, 1972: *Frank O'Farrell is sacked by Manchester United. Best once again announces his retirement from football*

Dec 21, 1972: *Sir Matt Busby is put in temporary charge. The United directors call a special meeting at the Cliff training ground to reassure players and staff about the future. Speculation that Wolves' Bill McGarry will take over is dismissed*

Dec 22, 1972: *Tommy Docherty agrees £15,000 a year deal to become new United manager*

Dec 23, 1972: *Man Utd 1, Leeds 1*

Dec 26, 1972: *Derby 3, Man Utd 1*

Jan 6, 1973: *Arsenal 3, Man Utd 1*

Jan 11, 1973: *Following an incident at Rubens nightclub, Best is found guilty of assaulting waitress Stefanja Sloniecka*

Jan 13, 1973: *Wolves 1, Man Utd 0 (FA Cup)*

Jan 20, 1973: *Man Utd 2, West Ham 2*

Jan 24, 1973: *Man Utd 0, Everton 0*

Jan 27, 1973: *Coventry 1, Man Utd 1*

Feb 10, 1973: *Man Utd 2, Wolves 1*

Feb 17, 1973: *Ipswich 4, Man Utd 1*

Feb 19, 1973: *Best is due to fly to Canada to discuss an offer to play in an indoor soccer league for £2,200 a game. But he is put off from flying out after receiving threats that he will be shot at Manchester airport*

Mar 3, 1973: *Man Utd 2, West Brom 1*

Mar 10, 1973: *Birmingham 3, Man Utd 1*

Mar 17, 1973: *Man Utd 2, Newcastle 1*

Mar 24, 1973: *Tottenham 1, Man Utd 1*

Mar 26, 1973: *Best says he would like to play for Northern Ireland but United say they would oppose the move*

Mar 31, 1973: *Southampton 0, Man Utd 2*

Apr 7, 1973: *Man Utd 1, Norwich 0*

Apr 11, 1973: *Man Utd 2, Crystal Palace 0*

Apr 14, 1973: *Stoke 2, Man Utd 2*

Apr 18, 1973: *Leeds 0, Man Utd 1*

Apr 21, 1973: Man Utd 0, Man City 0
Apr 23, 1973: Man Utd 1, Sheff Utd 2
Apr 25, 1973: Best meets up with
United boss Tommy Docherty and
agrees that his first game back in
action will be for Northern Ireland
against England on May 12. How he
performs in that game and also
against Scotland and Wales in the
Home Championships will determine
if and when he will return to League
soccer
Apr 26, 1973: Best returns to training
Apr 28, 1973: Chelsea 1, Man Utd 0
May 7, 1973: Best ends up in hospital
after suffering from thrombosis after
holiday in Marbella
May 8, 1973: Northern Ireland 3,
Cyprus 0 (World Cup qualifier)
June 19, 1973: Best again announces
that he is quitting the game. He also
reveals that he is planning a book
with Michael Parkinson
July 19, 1973: Manchester
magistrates refuse Best and business
colleagues a licence for the Jumbles
club, a planned nightclub in a
skyscraper
Aug 28, 1973: Best holds talks with
Manchester United and announces
that he would like to start playing
again

171

Eddie Hindle lives on the south coast of Spain with his Spanish partner.

Malcolm Wagner left Slack Alice's night club, opened Mr Thomas's Chop House and later ran the Grant Arms hotel and restaurant in Ramsbottom, which he sold. He is married, retired, lives in Manchester, plays golf and has written a book – *George Best and Me: Waggy's Tale* – in collaboration with Tom Page.

Frank O'Farrell became manager of Cardiff City in November, 1973. In April, 1974, he took charge of Iran before returning to the UK to manage Torquay in 1976. He retired from football in 1983 and continued living in Torquay.

"Che Sera," modified since George paid £30,000 to have the house built in 1970, is now owned by Harry Yeung, co-owner of the Yang Sing restaurant in Manchester city centre.

The Grapes pub is still in business in Little Quay Street. Pictures of pub owner Liz Dawn, the actress famous for her role as Vera Duckworth in TV soap Coronation Street, now adorn the wall alongside other celebrity pictures, including those of Sir Alex Ferguson, Eric Cantona and modern day United players paying a visit to George's old haunt.

Carolyn Moore is married and has a 32-year-old daughter.

Mrs Mary Fullaway died in March 1983, aged 74.

Frank Evans recently published a book, The Last British Bullfighter (2009), telling his colourful life story, including chapters on his time spent with George.

Martin Buchan inherited the captaincy from Bobby Charlton in 1973-74 but couldn't prevent United being relegated from the Second Division. He played more than 450 games for the club before leaving on a free transfer to Oldham after suffering a series of injuries. He led United to a famous FA Cup triumph against Liverpool in 1977, which denied the Merseysiders a famous Treble.

Ian Storey-Moore retired from football through injury in 1974. He scored 12 goals for United.

Paddy Crerand made 401 appearances for United. He still works in the media covering United.

Wyn Davies made 16 appearances for United, scoring four goals. He moved to Blackpool in 1973 before moving on to Stockport County, Crewe Alexandra and Bangor City.

Ted MacDougall scored five goals in 18 games for United but was shipped out to West Ham before the end of the season by Tommy Docherty.

Terry Neill continued to manage his country until 1975, hanging up his boots in 1973. He went on to manage Tottenham for a short spell and then became Arsenal's youngest manager in 1976, succeeding Bertie Mee at Arsenal. He was sacked in 1983.